DRUGS
WHAT YOUR KID SHOULD KNOW

a parent handbook by
K. Wayne Hindmarsh, PH.D.

DRUGS

WHAT YOUR KID
SHOULD KNOW

by

K. WAYNE HINDMARSH, PH.D.

Canadian Cataloguing in Publication Data

Hindmarsh, K. Wayne

   Drugs : What Your Kid Should Know

   3rd ed. —

   Includes bibliographical references.
   ISBN 0–9695996–0–9

1. Substance abuse. 2. Youth – Substance abuse.
I. Title.

HV5801.H55   1992   362.29'0835   C92–098048–1

PHARMACY
& APOTEX
CONTINUING
EDUCATION

A Pharmacy Service Program
from

To my wife, Lois and my children, Carla and Ryan. Without their encouragement and support, this handbook would not have been written.

CONTENTS

FOREWORD

This second printing is intended to serve as an updated educational tool for parents. It is true, there are many publications dealing with the subject of drug abuse but not many of them are truly comprehensive. Furthermore, many publications are written specifically for the professional and may be difficult to comprehend. A gap exists in the information available for the general public. This handbook has attempted to partially fill this gap. Attempts have been made to describe, in understandable terms, the potential health effects of drugs which are currently abused.

The author has taken care to provide accurate information, gathered from personal experience and from many sources within the scientific literature. A reference list has been included at the end of the handbook. Any reference which has been inadvertently omitted will be included in the next printing. It is not the intent of the author to claim the information as his own. The case studies used throughout the handbook, with the exception of two, were obtained from the medical literature. The names used are fictitious. Any similarity to known drug abusers is purely coincidental.

It is well known that informed parents are best equipped to prevent their children from becoming involved with drugs. This handbook will provide parents, youth and other consumers with up-to-date factual information on a wide group of drugs. After reading this handbook, the consumer will have a better grasp of the effects of the drugs our kids might be using and will thus be able to wisely counteract views put forth by "pro-drug activists." It is also hoped an understanding of the seriousness of drug abuse will lead to beneficial discussions among family members.

K. Wayne Hindmarsh, Ph.D.

ACKNOWLEDGEMENTS

This handbook exists as a result of the support and direction from many dedicated friends, family and colleagues. I wish to express my sincere appreciation to them all.

The drawings, interspersed through this handbook, were done by May Chow, a graduate of the College of Pharmacy, University of Saskatchewan, and now a practicing pharmacist in Regina, Canada. These excellent drawings visually reinforce the hazards associated with drug abuse. The greater part of the library research was done by Leanne Reimche, also a graduate of the College of Pharmacy, University of Saskatchewan, and now a medical student in British Columbia. Thank you so much May and Leanne for your hard work and valuable input!

I would particularly like to thank those members of my Advisory board who read the first draft and provided meaningful suggestions. These persons include Lois Hindmarsh, Dr. Dorothy Smith, Dr. Yvonne Shevchuk, Professor Ken Ready, Dr. E. Korchinski, Richard W. Muenz, Eloise Opheim, Shelly Porter-Serviss & David Wasylyshyn. I also wish to acknowledge the support of Dr. Thomas J. Gleaton, Governor General Ramon Hnatyshyn, Dean Jim Blackburn and the rest of my pharmacy colleagues.

A manuscript takes many hours of preparation. Without the typing skills of Zenia Dziadyk and Jackie Huck, the handbook would not have become a reality.

K.W. Hindmarsh
Faculty of Pharmacy
University of Manitoba
Winnipeg, Canada

INHALATION ABUSE

IT'S BETTER TO STOP AND
SMELL THE ROSES

INHALATION ABUSE

It's Better to 'Stop and Smell The Roses'

The concept of the popular song 'Stop and Smell The Roses' was good advice. Unfortunately, our society started smelling or inhaling other things which have led to serious life-threatening problems. Consider the following:

> *The body of an 8-year-old boy, Craig, was found frozen and tangled in a barbed wire fence. The only clues as to the cause of death were traces of a white substance in his nostrils. He had been sniffing typewriter correction fluid.*

> *Ted, a 16-year-old white boy, sat in a field with three other boys sniffing a cleaning fluid from a plastic bag. After 45 minutes of intermittent sniffing he jumped up, took off at a fast run for about 150 feet, and then collapsed. He was pronounced dead on arrival at the hospital.*

> *Mark, a 16-year-old Caucasian male, sprayed Arrid Extra-Dry deodorant into a plastic bag and took several deep breaths from the bag. He removed the bag from his face, grabbed one of his companions and said, 'Help me! Help me!' then collapsed. He was rushed to a local hospital where attempts at resuscitation were unsuccessful.*

Sudden deaths associated with 'sniffing' emphasize the seriousness of this type of abuse. There is such a fine line between inhaling enough solvent to obtain a high and inhaling too much and passing into unconsciousness. Common household products containing volatile solvents such as lacquer thinners, glues, nail polish remover, plastic cement and cooking

Is this the end?

sprays are capable of sensitizing the heart to a normal body chemical, epinephrine. Emotional stress and/or physical stress can cause the body to release extra amounts of epinephrine. This extra epinephrine makes the heart beat faster and faster to the point where the body cannot cope. Without medical treatment, the end result could be death due to fibrillation (rapid, randomized contractions) of the heart. The heart does not have enough time to properly fill with blood and cannot deliver adequate amounts of blood to the rest of the body.

The Problem in Perspective

Although sniffing or inhaling solvents is not new to society, the problem has spread since the first reports in the late 1950s. Serious physical and social problems can and do occur. For example, model cement inhalation can cause minor eye, nose and throat irritation but more seriously, muscle weakness which could lead to tremors, nervous system breakdown, liver, kidney and brain damage and heart abnormalities. In short, the most important organs of our body are seriously affected. Gasoline sniffing may result in lead poisoning, hallucinations, anemias where the blood forming functions of the body are seriously damaged, and even psychosis where an individual thinks people are 'out to get him or her.' The problems which occur are all serious but depend to some extent on the product being inhaled. Each product used by abusers contains different solvents or mixtures of solvents. From time to time manufacturers change the formula used for making their products. Sniffers are obviously not made aware of the changes. Abusers have suddenly become ill and had to be hospitalized after sniffing a product with a changed formulation.

Solvent abusers become lazy, apathetic and pre-occupied with obtaining their 'high.' Nothing else matters! Poor academic performance will be evident when they bring home a report card. Their group of friends will probably change, if they have any at all. The person becomes totally frustrated! Unfortunately, abusers do not always understand why things are going so poorly. Regular sniffers are often from unstable or broken homes, may have an alcoholic parent, will perform poorly in school, get into trouble with the law and have trouble coping with personal problems.

Despite the serious physical and social problems, lawmakers have not developed a uniform method for the control of the inhalation practice. Some merchants are forbidden to sell volatile products to minors yet, in other parts of North America, such action is not enforced. Consequently,

4

we find solvent abusers being referred for treatment and rehabilitation each year. Some of the young people being treated indicate there is a lot of 'sniffing' among their peers. There are parents who encourage and instruct their children to purchase or steal solvents for the family. Innocent victims are also being affected. Take, for example, a report of an infant being sedated with a solvent-dipped cloth, placed over the face, so the parents could sniff and drink in peace.

Solvent abuse has no respect for age, occupation or status. In some areas it has been estimated the prevalence of solvent use varies between 3.8% and 16.6% of the population. The lower the age and the grade, the greater the number of users! For instance one study found 3.7% of seventh graders used 'glue' while only 0.2% of thirteenth graders reported use.

Effects of Sniffing

Glue sniffing has a great hazard potential. A sniffer wants to achieve a state of euphoria, or simply 'a high,' but could rapidly lose consciousness and develop serious breathing problems with resulting damage to the brain and other body tissues. All of these factors may lead to death. The inhalation response develops progressively in four stages:

Stage 1: This excitatory stage gives one the feeling of 'floating on a cloud.' However, some experience dizziness, visual and hearing hallucinations, drooling, nausea, vomiting, flushed skin, abnormal intolerance to light and bizarre behaviour.

Stage 2: Includes symptoms such as confusion, disorientation, dullness, loss of self-control, ringing in the ears, blurred vision, double vision, cramps, headache and loss of pain sensitivity.

Stage 3: There is further reduction in arousal and coordination. The abuser will appear dazed, dopey and drowsy. There is muscular incoordination, slurred speech and depressed reflexes.

Stage 4: The sniffer may be in a state of stupor, delirium or unconsciousness and have bizarre dreams or epileptic-like seizures.

Obviously stage 1 is as far as 'sniffers' would like to go. Unfortunately, some do not stop at this stage.

The 1990s have seen an increase in butane and propane use. These substances can freeze the back of the throat, cause edema (collection of fluid) and cut the airway, i.e. the user chokes to death or suffocates.

Long-term Effects

The harmful effects of long-term solvent abuse have not been clearly defined. However, a number of complications have been seen. These include brain, kidney and liver damage, blood changes and disturbances to the nervous system. Some inhalers have had such serious nervous system damage that they became quadriplegic and will spend the rest of their lives in a wheelchair. Brain damage has been seen in both adults and children. An example of brain damage was seen in a 41-year-old woman who was admitted to hospital because she was 'losing her mind.'

> *For eight months, prior to admission, she had sniffed leaded gasoline three or four times a day. She would place her nose into the opening of a can containing the gasoline and inhale in an intermittent manner so that unconsciousness was avoided. She experienced a number of pleasant, as well as terrifying, events. She began to hallucinate and thought she was being used for brain experiments. She was convinced men had placed radar in her home to spy on her thoughts. She frequently had terrifying dreams and would awaken screaming that blood was oozing from her scalp.*
> *All these symptoms were traced to gasoline sniffing.*

Along with the serious problems resulting to the body from inhalation, a number of sniffers have suffered burn injuries from inhaling gasoline while smoking. Two examples are described by the following cases.

> *A 14-year-old girl was sniffing gasoline with friends in a car parked in front of her home. While she was holding the gasoline container between her legs one friend lit a cigarette. This caused an explosion which resulted in serious burns to all the occupants in the car.*

> *A 14-year-old boy skipped school and went with a friend to a wooded area to sniff gasoline. His friend bumped into him, causing some gasoline to spill on his clothing. Upon lighting a cigarette his body became a human torch!*

6

TOLERANCE: One tube isn't enough!

Many children have reported the development of tolerance to solvent fumes. This means an increase in the amount of product needed to achieve the effect originally felt on that first experience. For instance, one boy needed to inhale the vapors from 25 tubes of glue in order to achieve the effect he originally got from one tube. Another abuser was rescued after using 56 tubes of glue. This tolerance phenomenon is costly from a financial point of view and could lead to crime or prostitution in order the support the habit. If a tube of model cement costs $1.95, the boys using 25 and 56 tubes of glue would need between $48 and $109 for each sniffing session. This amount of money is considerably more than the average allowance for 12- to 14-year-old children! Why settle for glue when a gram of cocaine costs between $120–$250? Glue sniffers have been known to progress to other drugs of abuse—namely marijuana or Acid.

Products Used

Besides gasoline, a recent survey among retailers indicated the products most often abused include model airplaine glue, contact cements and adhesives, nail polish remover, aerosols, Lysol spray and hair sprays. Retail outlets report these products are difficult to keep in stock and the reason for their depletion is believed to be abuse. Other products such as deodorants, lighter fluid (butane), propane, spot removers, paint thinners, correction fluid and Rush (a volatile nitrite) are believed to be less commonly abused but virtually any product which contains a volatile solvent has been or will be abused.

Volatile Nitrites

Popping volatile nitrites by breaking their containers and sniffing them through the nose is also a popular fad. In the late 1960s, amyl nitrite (a blood vessel dilator) sales rose sharply due to its nonmedical use as an agent for getting 'high' and a substance for exciting sexual desire. The crushable amyl nitrite glass containers became known as 'poppers' to the drug culture and in the late 1970s other nitrites (e.g. butyl nitrites) became so popular that they accounted for sales of $50 million per year. These nitrites are sold over-the-counter as room deodorizers. Trade names include Rush, Macho, Aroma of Men, Locker Room, Bullet, Double Blast and Thrust. The products are inhaled directly from the bottle or by means of a single or double nasal inhaler. Some discotheques have even used special lighting effects to indicate they are about to spray nitrite fumes over the dance floor. This practice supposedly promotes a sense of abandon in dancing and stimulates music appreciation.

Chemically, nitrites are very unstable. Decomposition occurs at room temperature or if exposed to daylight. The nitrites, when inhaled or ingested, can readily induce changes in the ability of blood to carry oxygen due to an alteration in hemoglobin. Users may become cyanotic and their skin may take on a bluish color. Nitrites also cross the placental barrier in pregnant women and can produce blood changes in the fetus. Other toxic effects include: 'nitrite headaches,' lightheadedness, fainting, tolerance, lack of muscle control, delirium, a profound drop in blood pressure, skin flushing and transient heart changes. More seriously, inhaled nitrites are broken down in the body to a nitrite ion. This ion is a potential cancer-causing substance. Nitrites are also known to be immunosuppressant agents.

Nitrous Oxide

Inhalation of nitrous oxide for a pleasurable experience is common. The oxide has been referred to as 'a bag full of laughs,' the 'grocery-store high' and the 'lunch-hour drug.' A proprietor of a 'Head Shop' in Toronto viewed nitrous oxide as the ideal mind-altering substance for a hectic, urban environment where there is little time to drop out of reality. For seventy-five cents you could have some nitrous oxide transferred from a small metal canister into a balloon and the gas could be inhaled within the store. A 'high' lasts for one or two minutes.

Nitrous oxide has been appropriately used as an anesthetic during dental surgery. The occasional appropriate use when the dentist is visited will not cause serious health problems. The oxide has also been used so that whipping cream will rise. The gas has been viewed as being harmless. However, too much nitrous oxide, taken over an extended period of time, may lead to dullness, forgetfulness, difficulty in comprehending, brain damage and even death.

It is encouraging to note that 66% of retailers surveyed in a recent study thought they had an obligation to inform the public of the dangers of solvent-containing products. Unfortunately, a minority were found to be 'cashing-in' on the problem. In one community, one business was taking advantage of the solvent abuse situation by giving customers an extra can of Lysol spray as an incentive to shop at their store.

Although there are adults abusing solvents, the major problem is with the youth. Why they get involved has been a matter of speculation. It is a fact that a vast number initially try drugs or solvents with the false notion that they will not cause any harm and that they can be used safely. There is evidence to suggest that once a person gains an appreciation for the health hazards, his behaviour will change. One former solvent abuser emphatically stated she would never have tried it had she known the dangers.

In summary, the inhalation of volatile products is a dangerous practice. Serious health problems do occur. Some of these problems *cannot* be successfully treated! Life is like a game of chess. We have to watch every move or we may sacrifice our best man! **It's better to 'Stop and Smell The Roses.'**

Health Effects of Inhalation Abuse

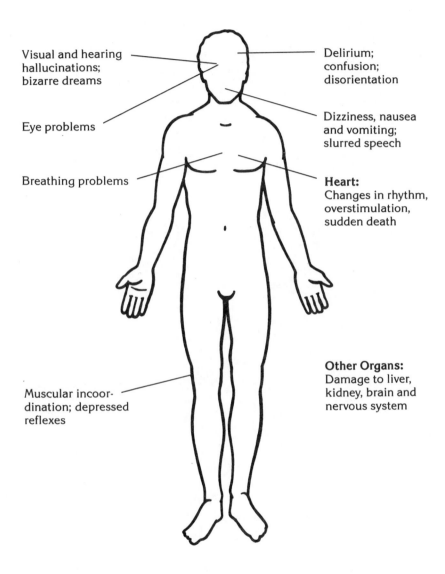

Visual and hearing hallucinations; bizarre dreams

Eye problems

Breathing problems

Muscular incoordination; depressed reflexes

Delirium; confusion; disorientation

Dizziness, nausea and vomiting; slurred speech

Heart:
Changes in rhythm, overstimulation, sudden death

Other Organs:
Damage to liver, kidney, brain and nervous system

- Loss of consciousness
- Skin flushing and irritation
- Ringing in the ears
- Epileptic-like seizures
- Cancer

- Immunosuppression
- Methemoglobinemia (a form of hemoglobin which cannot carry oxygen)

ALCOHOL

THE SIMPLE DRUG?

ALCOHOL
The Simple Drug?

How many times have you heard someone say after a wild party, "Thank goodness they were only drinking" or "It's too bad, but they're going to drink anyway and so it's not really a surprise"? This message seems to imply that alcohol is not as bad as other drugs which might have been involved. Alcohol is a 'simple drug,' at least from a chemical point of view. Its molecular formula is simple and easy to remember (CH_3CH_2OH). It is probably safe to assume that if this simple drug were discovered today, it probably would not be legalized. Alcohol has ruined lives, caused deaths and is responsible for millions of dollars of costs in health care budgets. Education has had considerable influence in informing the public as to the consequences of using, and in particular abusing, this so-called simple(?) drug, but there is still more to be done. Statistics continue to show alcohol is still the NUMBER ONE drug of abuse in youth. Yes, alcohol IS a drug—just like heroin, marijuana, cocaine or prescription drugs. The following true cases are good examples of problems associated with alcohol abuse.

Barbara, a 12-year-old girl, was admitted to the hospital with a three-hour history of vomiting after which she passed out. Upon arrival at the hospital she appeared drowsy but responded to the questions of the physician. She denied use of alcohol or other drugs and no alcohol was detected on her breath. However, laboratory results confirmed a blood alcohol concentration of 0.21%, i.e. in each 100 ml of blood there was 210 mg of alcohol. In other words this represents a Breathalyser reading of 0.21 (legal limit in Canada, 0.08). Barbara only then admitted to drinking gin and tonic with her friends.

Brian, a 10-year-old boy, was heard calling from the bathroom one night. His father, responding quickly to his cries, found his son drowsy, confused and frothing at the mouth. After some time Brian's condition worsened to a point of vomiting. He was quickly transported to the hospital. Although he was quite drowsy when he arrived, he was able to respond to commands. When questioned about the possibility of alcohol or drug inges- tion, both were denied. However, a laboratory determination revealed an alcohol level of 0.11%.

Brad, a 17-year-old teenager, had been drinking heavily over a four-month period. He apparently consumed large quantities of beer (up to 5 litres) and wine daily. Suddenly, he decided to discontinue his abusive habit and within 10 days began to experience bizarre behaviour (eye blinking and rolling, neck snapping, facial contortions, shoulder shrugging) and became very talkative. On medical examination it appeared these signs were due to alcohol withdrawal (a term used to describe the symptoms seen on sudden stoppage of drinking alcohol). Many of the signs disappeared within one month, however, he con- tinued to experience occasional eye blinking and shoulder shrugging for some time.

Alcohol in Perspective

A number of agencies have conducted drug prevalence surveys in an attempt to follow trends. A 1991 survey of over 10,000 Canadian youth in grades 6–13, conducted by PRIDE CANADA (Parent Resources Institute for Drug Education), revealed that 76.5% of the senior high school students drank beer within the last year, while 67.8% drank wine and 74.4% drank liquor. So what? These students, for the most part are *under the legal drink- ing age!* The statistics were further defined to determine heavy use of alcohol. Drinking alcohol one to seven times a week is considered heavy use. In other words, it is not just the occasional drink! The results were high: 30.0% of grade 12 students reported heavy use of beer; 20.0% reported heavy use of liquor; 10.0% of the grade 9 students reported heavy use of beer; 7.5% reported heavy liquor use. It may be argued that drinking once a week is hardly considered heavy use but keep in mind that young people generally drink to get a 'buzz.' Each drinking episode is more than just one bottle or can of the foaming liquid. A significant increase in the reported heavy consumption of alcohol between eighth and ninth grades was also noted in the above study. In some parts of Canada, ninth grade is the first exposure to high school and the 'big boys'!

The legal drinking age varies from country to country and within countries. For example, the legal drinking age in the United States is 21, while in Canada some provinces have set the legal age at 18 years and others at 19. Why is there a legal drinking age? The reasons are often forgotten. It's not to create jobs for the police and court personnel. To put it simply, alcohol is not tolerated well by young people. Some provinces in Canada tried lowering the drinking age with the hope that, if it were legal to drink, less alcohol would be consumed. In other words, there would not be the same challenge or thrill in trying something illegal. The experiment failed! Alcohol consumption and the problems associated with its use increased. Unfortunately, the beverage chosen by youth is not just beer. The term 'just beer' is deceiving since one beer has just as much alcohol as one shot of liquor—in other words, beer can produce the same effects as liquor and wine. Liquor or 'hard stuff' is also being used excessively, as seen from the results of the above survey.

Alcohol is a 'gateway drug.' That is, persons who drink are more prone to use other drugs than those who do not drink. Drinking doesn't necessarily lead to the use of other drugs, but the possibility exists. Also, it has been reported that those who drink regularly at age 16 have a higher probability of becoming heavy drinkers in their twenties.

Are adults to blame for the excessive use of alcohol by youth? If they do not provide clear-cut reasons for not drinking, the answer is yes. Young people look to adults and parents for guidance. Even though young people may not always agree with the guidelines imposed, parents who do take a stand are respected. Adults who do not agree with the drinking age imposed by their government should insist on an open forum. The debate would be interesting. The legal drinking age could rise!

Short-term Effects of Alcohol

Alcohol is consumed primarily for its euphoric (feeling of well-being or elation) and intoxicating effects. As a result there is the misconception that alcohol is a stimulant. Alcohol has just the opposite effect and is actually a depressant that depresses brain function. While some people may become more sociable, others turn moody and obnoxious. The latter effect is often not perceived by the drinking person. As alcohol intake increases,

Sociability?

more of the brain is affected. The eventual outcome is sleep, breathing difficulties and, more seriously, death.

Any alcohol consumption has an effect on one's judgement and self-control. These functions are impaired long before physical incoordination is apparent. Friends might not realize the problem and may misjudge the ability of their buddy to drive. The truth is, any alcohol ingestion may be too much for some to safely drive a motor vehicle. This is particularly true for young people. The effects of alcohol on their judgement are more pronounced. A young person likes to experience a 'buzz'—it goes along with a good time. Driving a vehicle definitely should not be attempted at this stage.

A number of programs have been developed to cut down on the number of motor vehicle accidents. SADD (Students Against Driving Drunk) is a good example. Many SADD chapters have been formed in North America. Anything that can be done to prevent one of the major effects of alcohol in teens (death or permanent damage, such as quadriplegia or permanent paralysis) is worthwhile. *BUT* the attitude that young people *will* drink has to be addressed! Young people should grow up drug-free, not with the attitude that a designated driver is there to support them. Youth groups are mutiplying across North America which support the 'drug-free' concept. PRIDE is only one example. Adults should do all they can to support them. It's time to dispel the beliefs that nothing will work. If the youth do not get the support they need from adults this is what will happen.

Television portrays 'good times' associated with drinking. Unfortunately this is not the case as many will verify. Accidents and violence are serious problems. Fights, break-ins and other crimes are the result of altered reasoning ability caused by alcohol. Some rape victims are unable to defend themselves because they are themselves, under the influence of alcohol at the time of attack. Too often we excuse people for what they have done because they were 'under the influence at the time.' This is a mistake!

How Alcohol Works

Medically speaking, alcohol acts on a system of nerve cells known as the 'reticular formation' which is located in the brain stem. When stimuli such as sound and pain act on the body, information is sent to the brain in the form of coded electrical impulses. These prompt the brain to identify the information and match it with memory. This identification initiates a response. Alcohol, even in small doses, suppresses this matching process.

18

Individuals become less attentive and are preoccupied with their inner thoughts and emotions and a response may not be initiated or, if initiated, the response or reaction time is slow.

The liver is an important organ. Humans cannot survive without it. Any substance taken orally passes through the liver before it reaches the blood stream. Substances are 'screened' by the liver and are seen as being something useful for the body, something that could be useful if converted into some other chemical structure or something which should be eliminated. In order for a drug to be eliminated from the body, the liver will convert it to something that is easily excreted, i.e. will be eliminated through the urine or feces. Alcohol is eliminated primarily by chemical structural changes occurring in the liver. In fact, alcohol is eventually converted into carbon dioxide and water. It is eliminated at a constant rate, that is, blood concentrations decrease by a constant amount every hour. Blood alcohol concentrations decrease, on average, by 0.015% per hour, after drinking has ceased. The elimination of alcohol from blood cannot be speeded up by taking a cold shower, drinking black coffee or by any other means your friends might suggest. If sufficient alcohol is ingested during an 'evening out' with friends, it is possible to be still legally drunk the next morning. The alcohol has not been completely removed from the body during the few hours of sleep and the blood level is not below the legal limit of 0.05 or 0.08. This fact should be kept in mind when getting behind the wheel of an automobile the next morning.

Long-term Effects of Alcohol

Some of the long-term effects of alcohol (effects seen after drinking alcohol for an extended period of time, i.e. months or years) may also be seen on short-term use (weeks or months). Therefore, don't think the following problems will not occur with just the occasional drink.

Effects on the Gastrointestinal Tract (Stomach and Intestine)

Food taken into the body has to be broken down and digested. Alcohol is absorbed directly, without being broken down, through the walls of the stomach and the small intestine. Approximately 20–30% is absorbed through the stomach and the remainder through the small intestine. Once alcohol has moved into the blood, it is distributed throughout the body, including the brain, depending on water content. Alcohol irritates the lining of the stomach and intestine causing a breakdown of the protective lining (mucosa). Noticeable effects would include heartburn or more serious pain. The seriousness increases with the amount of alcohol consumed and with the concentration of alcohol in the drink. The walls of the stomach become inflamed which generally results in pain. If drinking continues, bleeding, ulcers and perforation (hole) of the stomach may result. Loss of blood, if excessive, is serious.

Effects on the Liver

The cases of liver cirrhosis (inflammation) diagnosed in North America are, for the most part, a result of heavy alcohol use. Alcohol and its breakdown products (metabolites) are toxic (poisonous) to the liver. Heavy consumption is often used as a substitute for food. The lack of vitamin and nutrient intake means the liver does not have the proper nutrients to function normally. For example, vitamin K, a necessary substance for the clotting process of blood, cannot be utilized and the alcoholic is thus known as a 'potential bleeder'. Furthermore, the damaged liver is unable to utilize sugar, proteins or fats to their fullest potential. Blood sugar levels may thus become dangerously low (hypoglycemia).

Effects on the Heart

Alcohol is a poison to muscle fibre. The heart is a muscle. Combined with vitamin deficiencies and other problems associated with alcohol use, heart muscle is weakened or destroyed. Anyone suffering from a heart condition will find that alcohol makes it worse and could precipitate a fatal heart attack. Perhaps most significant is the effect of alcohol on blood pressure. Men and women who have a daily drinking routine (more than three drinks) tend to have higher blood pressure than non-drinkers. Alcohol has, therefore, been included as a risk factor that can lead to hypertension. Doctors will tell patients with high blood pressure that they should stop smoking and drinking.

Effects on the Muscles

As described for the heart, alcohol weakens muscles. Muscle tremor, muscle incoordination and an increase in reaction time occur (i.e.

the individual takes longer to react). This is a very important factor to keep in mind when driving a car and operating machinery . . . **don't do it while under the influence of alcohol!**

Effects on the Blood

The poor eating habits of the alcohol user result in vitamin deficiencies. A drink often takes the place of a well-balanced meal. The resulting vitamin deficiencies have a profound effect on all parts and functions of the body. The list of medical blood problems resulting from alcohol abuse is long. A reduction in red blood cells (anemia), white blood cells and platelets has been reported, leading to an increased risk of infection and blood clotting problems.

Effects on Hormone Levels

Alcohol produces a drop or fall in the male hormone, testosterone. Testosterone, familiar to everyone, is the hormone responsible for the remarkable changes during puberty that transform a boy into a man. Testosterone levels will usually return to normal fairly rapidly after the cessation of drinking, however, continued use produces consistent low levels of the hormone. In the male, this can produce feminine features such as breast growth, decreased body hair and reduced beard growth. In addition, there is decreased sexual drive and impotence. Prostate problems may also develop because the gland decreases in size and its function is inhibited.

The effects to the female are serious but not as visually evident. Alcohol does interfere with the menstrual cycle as a result of change in ovary function. The outcome might be sterility and early onset of menopause.

Effects on Pregnancy

Alcohol, being a small molecule, readily crosses the placenta, reaching the fetus and affecting its development. Physical and mental deficiencies have been observed in the newborn. These symptoms are referred to as Fetal Alcohol Syndrome (FAS). Body size of the offspring is decreased compared to normal infants, the brain is smaller and there are varying degrees of mental retardation. Facial symptoms include retardation in the growth of the jaw, an upturned nose, thin lips and abnormal facial skin folds.

Alcohol and pregnancy.

Heart defects (murmurs) and skeletal abnormalities leading to limited joint movements have also been observed.

Women who consider themselves only social or moderate drinkers can still put the fetus at risk, but the symptoms are usually less severe than those of FAS. Any alcohol consumption can affect the fetus. The fetus progresses through many developmental stages. Some of these stages are more sensitive to the effect of drugs, including alcohol, than others. The thalidomide tragedy is a good example of what a drug can do if taken at the wrong time during pregnancy. Many babies, born to mothers who took thalidomide during their pregnancy, had 'seal-like' appendages (flippers) rather than arms and hands. So many intricate processes occur during the development of the fetus that it is wise to avoid anything that might interfere with these stages.

The use of alcohol has been linked to sexual activity and disinhibition. There certainly have been unwanted pregnancies resulting from sexual encounters while under the influence of alcohol. A study in Scotland showed that almost 50% of males and females had consumed alcohol before their first experience of sexual intercourse, and those who had taken a drink were much less likely to have used condoms. Thus alcohol could be considered a risk factor with respect to AIDS and other sexually transmitted diseases.

Effects on the Nervous System

Most people are aware that the nervous system is affected by alcohol use. The symptoms of delirium tremens (DTs) are fairly well known as they are frequently portrayed by the movie industry. The symptoms are pronounced and are due to the fact that alcohol is no longer present and the brain has become accustomed to its presence. The brain responds by initiating trembling, excitement, anxiety, sweating, difficulty in sleeping, increased body temperature, increased heart rate and pain. These effects begin to occur two to four days after cessation of drinking or may result simply from a reduced blood alcohol level in the alcoholic who can't get his usual supply or is injured or catches an infection. The body is not able to handle the physical stress. A significant percentage of patients with DTs die.

Inflammation of nerves from continued alcohol consumption produces a burning and prickly sensation in the hands and feet. The actual cause is probably a vitamin deficiency (poor diet). In fact, vitamin deficiencies are responsible for a significant number of the problems.

Effects on the Brain

Serious brain damage produces syndromes, referred to as Wernicke syndrome and Korsakoff's psychosis (mental disorders). The syndromes are named after the scientists who discovered them. When one reaches the stage of Wernicke syndrome, drinking has been over an extended period of time (months or years). The Wernicke syndrome is characterized by confusion, difficulty in controlling eye and leg muscles and, if untreated, progresses to the more serious Korsakoff's psychosis which is characterized by memory loss. Psychosis means there is brain cell loss and damage to the brain structure. Korsakoff's psychosis is difficult to treat and might be considered untreatable.

Effects on the Mouth, Throat and Lungs

Continued use of alcohol increases the incidence of cancer of the mouth, throat and lungs. Cancer of these areas represents a significant proportion of all cancers detected in the white and black populations.

Tolerance and Dependence

As alcohol use continues, the body adapts to and needs more alcohol to produce the effect felt with that first drink. This phenomenon is known as 'tolerance.' People adapt to the continued depressant effects on the brain and gradually more alcohol is required before one appears drunk.

As with other drugs, both physical and psychological dependence to alcohol develops. Physical dependence is seen, in its worst scenario, by delirium tremens (DTs). As described in the case study at the beginning of this chapter, Brad was physically dependent. When one feels he/she must have the drug in order to survive or to be 'on top of things'—psychological dependence has occurred.

Underage Drinking

It takes between 7 to 15 years for an adult male to become an alcoholic and between 5 to 12 years for an adult female. Few are aware that young people can become alcoholics much quicker. The average time is between 2 to 5 years. However, some have become alcoholics in just a few **months.**

Adult lack of concern.

> *Alcoholism has been defined as 'a chronic disorder in which the individual is unable, for physical or psychological reasons, or both, to refrain from frequent consumption of alcohol in quantities sufficient to produce intoxication and ultimately, injury to health and functioning.'*

Treatment centres are now admitting significantly more teenage alcoholics. A young developing body simply has difficulty handling alcohol. The growing tissues and cells are more prone to the cellular poison (alcohol) than are mature adult tissues. Unfortunately, after people reach the so-called 'magic age' when it is legal to drink, a significant number still cannot handle alcohol, but society is saying you should now be able to make your own decisions and feels you are mature enough to make the right choice.

Young people have many reasons for drinking: curiosity, peer pressure, as a crutch during emotional upheavals and yes, because they want to behave like an adult.

What kind of message are adults giving young people? Is there any thought given to the consequences of their actions? How about graduation parties? Do the parties include alcohol, even though the students are underage? If so, why? Is it a fear of 'not being cool' or of being ridiculed? These parties create further peer pressure. Students are being pressured into attending a party which they normally might not attend simply because no alternatives are provided. The stage is set for a young person to take a drink. No one wants to be left out or feel like he doesn't belong!

If parents do not realize it is possible to celebrate without alcohol the battle against drug abuse will never be won. Parents in North America who have taken the challenge and who have worked hard in creating drug-free parties for youth are to be commended. Alcohol is a 'gateway' drug, which means it can lead to use of other drugs. It is a fact that most who use illegal drugs started with alcohol.

Is alcohol a **'simple'** drug? The evidence has been in for some time and the answer is **no!**

Health Effects of Alcohol Abuse

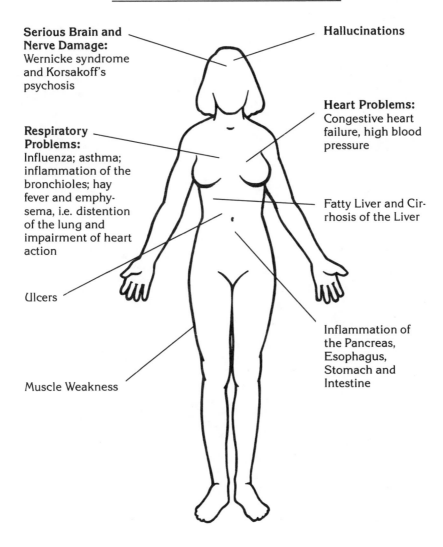

Serious Brain and Nerve Damage: Wernicke syndrome and Korsakoff's psychosis

Hallucinations

Respiratory Problems: Influenza; asthma; inflammation of the bronchioles; hay fever and emphysema, i.e. distention of the lung and impairment of heart action

Heart Problems: Congestive heart failure, high blood pressure

Fatty Liver and Cirrhosis of the Liver

Ulcers

Muscle Weakness

Inflammation of the Pancreas, Esophagus, Stomach and Intestine

- blood disorders including anemia
- diarrhea
- low blood sugar (hypoglycemia)
- low blood calcium levels (hypocalcemia)
- bronchitis and pneumonia

- tremors
- seizures
- nutritional disorders and deficiencies
- cancer
- infections of all types

MARIJUANA

THE 'DOPE' ON MARIJUANA

MARIJUANA

The 'Dope' on Marijuana

The terminology **'gone to pot,'** although often used to describe the physical shape of our bodies, can be quite appropriately used to describe those who have begun using the drug *marijuana* ('pot'). The use of marijuana has been extensively documented for years but only recently have the harmful effects on the body received attention. Serious physical and psychological effects are now being reported with regular and chronic use. In fact, scientists are now suggesting marijuana is more destructive to the brain than any other drug, with the exception of PCP (phencyclidine) and the latter stages of alcoholism.

The following true cases describe the effects marijuana can have on the human.

Tom, a likeable, attractive, well-mannered, intelligent grade 10 student, was liked by both his teachers and fellow students. His younger brother, Jim, similar to Tom, was in grade 8. Both were very involved in school and community sports including hockey, soccer, baseball and football.

To everyone's dismay, at Christmas time in grade 11, Tom was expelled from school for his involvement in a drug distribution ring that operated within his school. Tom's specific involvement was the distribution of marijuana and its products, namely hashish oil (the more concentrated form of the plant) and hashish cubes, as well as the plant material itself, to his fellow classmates. The distribution system was so widespread that no other school in the city, including private schools, would accept Tom as a student as they were all aware of his activities. Consequently, Tom never finished high school.

Tom had come under suspicion when his grades began to drop with no identifiable cause. The friends with whom he associated also changed over the summer holidays to those who lacked respect for school authority. His attentiveness subsequently declined and he would show up late for classes or not show at all. Involvement in sports activities also dropped markedly. On the other hand, Jim remained in the background when it came to Tom's drug involvement. He participated only as a user rather than as a distributor.

Tom and Jim are now adults. Tom is not married and is working in construction. Jim is also in a construction trade, but is divorced and has a young daughter. Jim met his wife among a drug-using crowd. She became pregnant when both of them were heavily involved in marijuana use. Their daughter, Susan, when born, appeared to be a normal, bright, healthy baby and her first few years of growth appeared uneventful. Susan is now in school and is having difficulty learning and socialising. According to her teachers she tends to be a loner. Even her grandparents notice a significant change in her attitude toward them. Tom continues to use marijuana products on a fairly regular basis, always striving to find the best available products; products of high quality and potency. He is no longer able to carry on an intelligent conversation.

Paul, a 20-year-old man, had just recently graduated 'cum laude' in Business Administration. He had been working in the family business and, before his experience with marijuana, was well adjusted both in his job and social life. Although Paul only smoked marijuana twice during his college days, he soon found his way into the 'in crowd' and began to smoke regularly. This habit immediately began to produce changes in his working pattern and a decline in ambition. The situation worsened to the point of apathy and distrust of friends and family.

Six months after starting to regularly smoke marijuana Paul developed delusions of omnipotence ('holier than thou') and grandeur ('there is no one quite as good as I'). He believed he was in charge of the mafia and he was a necessary supporter of the 'Ku Klux Klan.' He began to collect guns and knives, and trained his German shepherd dog to attack others. Finally, for fear he was losing his mind, Paul sought psychiatric treatment.

31

> *Upon discontinuing the use of the drug his fantasies disappeared. However, two years following treatment, Paul was still experiencing difficulty in thinking clearly.*

> *David, an outgoing 19-year-old teenager, had many friends and did well academically in school. Following only four months of marijuana use, he experienced a sharp decline in his interest for school work. He became listless, apathetic and depressed. He shunned family and friends and gradually developed ideas of reverence.*
> *Believing he had superhuman powers, he felt able to communicate with and control the minds and actions of animals, especially dogs and cats. Although he admitted these were weird ideas, he considered them to be true and believed marijuana was his source of power.*
> *Fortunately, when psychiatric help was sought and marijuana smoking discontinued, David returned to a level of functioning similar to that before marijuana use.*

Each year thousands of adolescents and adults are experimenting with marijuana with the false impression that it will do no harm. There is the false belief use can be controlled! Contrary to popular belief, marijuana IS a dangerous drug and continued use could have serious consequences on the normal functioning of the body.

What is Marijuana?

Marijuana, hash (also known as hashish) and hash oil are all derived from the *Cannabis* plant. The North American variety, *Cannabis sativa,* is a fibre-like plant with a well recognized jagged leaf. Two other marijuana plants include; *Cannabis indica,* found primarily throughout Asia, and a fast growing variety, *Cannabis ruderalis* (the 'super' strain), found in the Confederation of Independent States (C.I.S.). The three plant sources have similar constituents and thus have the same effect on the human body.

To date 421 chemicals have been reportedly found in the marijuana plant. On smoking a marijuana cigarette ('joint') chemical reactions take place, giving rise to an estimated total of 2000 compounds. Unfortunately, the effects of these compounds, when inhaled, is not known. It is frightening to even try to guess what the inhalation of 2000 foreign compounds could do to the body. Over 60 of the 421 compounds found in a joint are collectively known as cannabinoids, the major one being THC (tetrahydrocannabinol or delta 9-THC). THC is the cannabinoid responsible for the 'high.' Related compounds CBN (cannabinol) and CBD (cannabidiol) also have biological activity but the mind altering effects are not like those obtained from THC.

The potency of marijuana bought on the streets is determined by the THC content. During the late sixties and seventies, THC content was low—approximately one-half percent. In the 1980s it was not uncommon to find marijuana containing as much as 8% to 9% THC (some reported as high as 15%). In other words, marijuana of the 90s is much more potent and, more seriously, is being used by a younger age group. Just stop to think about it for a moment...public school children are inhaling 2000 chemicals from a more potent plant source. Why are there so many so-called 'experts' who want to decriminalize the 'weed'?

Potency or concentration increase of THC in the marijuana plant is partially due to crossbreeding (similar to the process which gives better wheat crops) and improved growing techniques, including hydroponics (growing plants in nutrient solutions, with or without soil). Unfortunately, it is now possible to grow the plant in your home, garage or in some other secluded spot.

Although the dangers of using marijuana are often attributed to the THC content, there are other constituents which are of equal concern. These include the tar and cancer-causing constituents found in the joint. *Cannabis* produces 50% more tar than the same weight of a popular brand tobacco cigarette. How many filter tip joints have you seen? The tar contains more than 150 polynuclear aromatic hydrocarbons, including the same cancer-causing agents found in cigarettes. One of these hydrocarbons is known as benzo[a]pyrene. The concentration of this component in marijuana tar is reportedly 70% higher than in the same weight of tobacco tar.

How is Marijuana Used?

Marijuana is most often smoked as a joint (cigarette). The joint contains ground-up plant material, leaves and seeds. Occasionally marijuana is consumed by eating food to which the drug has been added. Brownies have been known to contain hashish. A number of years ago a cookbook appeared on the streets which contained recipes that required

The potency of today's marijuana.

the inclusion of marijuana constituents. Interestingly, the book ended with a page explaining what to do if too much was consumed, i.e. a remedy for an overdose!

Marijuana is also used in the more concentrated form, 'hash' or 'hashish.' This concentrate, usually sold as a 'cube,' is dark brown to black in colour and contains, conservatively, 12% to 15% or more THC. Hashish is actually a resinous material secreted onto the surface of the plant. In some parts of the world women used to be in charge of collecting this resin. Wearing leather aprons they would run up and down the fields so the resin would stick to the aprons. The resin would then be scraped off with a knife. This is, of course, not a very sanitary process. Hash and hash oil have frequently been used to lace cigarettes or joints. Hash is also smoked using a pipe (which may or may not be a water pipe) or a bong (a large diameter tube device used to mix air with the smoke, thereby cooling the smoke prior to inhalation). Because the smoke from hash is very irritating to the throat, water or air is used to cool the smoke and relieve some of this irritation.

The highest concentration of THC is found in hash oil. This oil is obtained by percolation (a process similar to that used to make tea or coffee in a drip-percolator). Injection of hash oil is not a common practice because the method poses serious health problems: blood clots from foreign particles in the injected material and numerous diseases as a result of using dirty needles and syringes. Injecting hash oil is truly 'Russian roulette'! Hash oil may be added to cigarettes or joints.

Marijuana Distribution in the Body

THC and the other cannabinoids found in the marijuana plant are highly fat soluble; that is, they behave like an oil. The cannabinoids rapidly enter fat tissues of the body, but leave very slowly! The term 'fat heads,' although not a term of endearment, is really quite descriptive. Brain tissue is composed of considerable fat and marijuana 'loves' to spend time in this part (as well as other areas) of our body. Chronic or regular users of marijuana have been shown to have 50% *or less* brain cell energy than the amount seen in individuals who have not used the drug. Because cells are surrounded with lipid (fat soluble) material, THC eventually buries itself within every cell in the body. THC actually buries itself between the molecules which make up the membranes. As marijuana intake continues, the pores within these membranes become clogged. Clogged cells have difficulty functioning properly. Vital substances normally taken up by the cells cannot get in and substances normally released by the cells are not able to be released. One such substance is calcium. Calcium is one chemical substance which assists the intake of other substances required for the proper nourishment of the cells. If calcium's function is inhibited, neuro-transmitter (chemical substance necessary for the stimulation of other cells) release is inhibited, i.e. brain processes are inhibited and, to put it bluntly—**the user becomes dumber and dumber with continued use!** THC stays in the fat tissues for days. In fact, scientists have been able to detect constituents of marijuana in the body for up to one month after smoking one joint. The weekend user is thus actually accumulating marijuana constituents in the body. This means that what was inhaled last Saturday hasn't completely left the body by the following Saturday!

Marijuana Effects on Cell Function

The human body is composed of billions of cells. Human growth and development are dependent upon continual cellular growth and regeneration. THC and other cannabinoids inhibit this cellular growth rate by 8% to 55%, depending on the concentration of THC found in the plant material. It is a well-known fact that growing cells are more prone to toxic effects of chemicals than are mature cells. This means that young people are particularly vulnerable and damage to nervous system cells is often irreversible, i.e. these cells do not regenerate. On the other hand, some of the damage may be subtle, resulting in only minor defects which are not fatal to the cell. However, there are times when the cell actually dies or turns into a potential cancer cell.

Marijuana Effects on the Immune System

Marijuana impairs the functioning of 'T-cells.' These cells are important for normal functioning of the immune system. The AIDS virus kills 'T-cells,' thereby leaving the individual susceptible to serious life-threatening complications. Marijuana not only affects the 'T-cells' but also 'B-cells' (cells which produce antibodies). With these two cell types impaired, the defense system of the body is severely hampered and has difficulty fighting infections.

Our bodies have a certain number of precancerous cells. Fortunately, the immune system recognizes these cells and destroys them. An impaired immune system obviously reduces the efficiency with which these precancerous cells are destroyed, thereby increasing the risk of cancer.

Marijuana Effects on the Reproductive System

Tissue surrounding the testes in the male is very high in fat content. Accumulation of marijuana constituents in this part of the body decreases the production of testosterone, the male hormone.

It has been reported that levels of testosterone are decreased by as much as 35% within hours after smoking only one joint. Following the cessation of smoking, the testosterone levels will begin to return to normal unless the user is a chronic smoker. The male who has not reached puberty will find that the decrease in testosterone results in a delay in developing secondary sex characteristics, i.e. a deepening of the voice, growth of body hair on the face, groin and armpit areas. Low testosterone levels may also result in enlargement of the breasts. This would likely prove embarrassing to the male ego.

Sperm production also decreases in the marijuana user. The decreased sperm count and the decreased motility of the sperm partially explain the decreased fertility of the male marijuana user. Couples who want to have children may not be able to, but more frightening is the possibility of transmitting defective genetic material from the male to the offspring. Birth defects are possible. Remember, the father contributes one-half of the genes to the fetus!

The female is also affected by marijuana use. Ovaries have a fat content much like that of the testes. The female hormones, estrogen and progesterone, are affected by marijuana. Hormone disruption may mean testosterone levels in the female may become disproportionally high resulting in excess hair growth on her body and a deepening of the voice. The female menstrual cycle is often disrupted and anovulatory cycles (a time when an egg is not released by the ovaries) may result in temporary infertility.

The female begins life with one set of eggs which begin to mature at puberty. These eggs are very sensitive to chemical toxins and since the eggs are immature, they are more prone to toxic effects of chemicals. If damage occurs, it is permanent and may affect any baby the woman may have in later life. THC will cross the placenta and accumulate in the brain of the developing fetus (baby). This is probably what happened to Susan in the scenario at the beginning of this chapter. Need we say more?

Marijuana migration to the brain.

Marijuana Effects on the Heart

Marijuana causes an increase in heart rate. For the healthy individual this may not be serious. Those with heart problems will find marijuana makes matters worse. Blood pressure changes have also been reported, however, the long-term effects of marijuana on blood pressure are not known.

Marijuana Effects on the Pulmonary System

Because marijuana is most often smoked and inhaled there has been considerable investigation into its effect on the lungs. Marijuana smoke is usually deeply inhaled to allow for maximum absorption and effect. The bronchial injury caused by just four joints per week are reported to be equivalent to smoking sixteen tobacco cigarettes per day.

Lung damage may first appear as a sore throat, sometimes referred to as 'hash throat'. Irritation of the bronchial mucosa (lining) can lead to inflammation of the lungs (bronchitis). If bronchitis progresses this, along with excess mucous production, will lead to airway obstruction, emphysema (a disease that causes distension of the lung and frequently impairment of heart action) and permanent lung disease.

Marijuana Effects on the Brain

High-powered microscopic examination of brain tissue, taken during an autopsy, has shown marijuana constituents accumulate in a communication junction between nerve cells. This slows down the flow of information and increases the distance between the nerve cells. This effect appears to be permanent. Regardless of how little or how infrequently you may use marijuana 'it all adds up.' If used long enough an Organic Brain Syndrome could develop. This syndrome has many symptoms—lack of motivation, apathy and impairment of short-term memory. As a result some have difficulty getting their lives back together after long-term use. We have only one brain. A brain scan of a marijuana user might be most convincing. Paul (see beginning of this chapter) had fuzzy thinking for two years after using the drug. This 'fuzzy' thinking was due, at least partially, to the accumulation of marijuana in the brain.

Because the user's thought process is slowed down after using marijuana, under no circumstances should he drive a motor vehicle. A number of motor vehicle accidents have undoubtedly been caused by marijuana. Forensic laboratories have frequently found marijuana in the bodies of motor vehicle fatality victims. The federal government of Canada has recently established a 'Drugs and Driving Committee' to look into the involvement of drugs and their effect on the ability to drive. One issue of particular interest to this committee is the involvement of marijuana in drug fatalities and injuries.

Cannabis Syndrome and Psycho-social Effects

The effects of marijuana on the brain result in serious problems for the user. Cannabis syndrome or 'Marijuanism' is a common clinical entity. Doctors are seeing the symptoms more frequently during routine patient medicals. They report seeing patients with decreased motivation, shortened attention and concentration spans, lack of interest in the world around them, limited range of thought and feeling, inability to prepare realistically for the future, unrealistic thinking, impaired communication skills and general apathy. It is sad to see young people behave in this manner. Their whole life is ahead of them and they 'could care less'! Because of these effects, it is not uncommon for them to lose friends, drop out of school, lose jobs, and fight with their families. Marijuana users could, very quickly, become a *cost to society* as they can no longer function normally. It is very difficult to go back to school and try to catch up with what should have been learned years back. It's a vicious circle! Lack of education—no job!

Marijuana ('pot') can hardly be considered a drug which is safe to use. The above 'dope' on this drug shows that use can lead to permanent damage not only to the users but possibly to their offspring. The drug has been inappropriately referred to as a soft drug. The effects on the human body are not soft! The effects are cold, hard facts. **Don't let yourself 'go to pot'!**

Health Effects of Marijuana Use

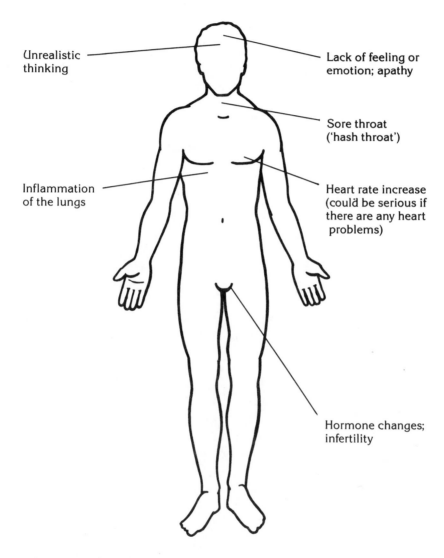

Unrealistic thinking

Lack of feeling or emotion; apathy

Sore throat ('hash throat')

Inflammation of the lungs

Heart rate increase (could be serious if there are any heart problems)

Hormone changes; infertility

- Inhibition of cell growth
- Nervous system damage (may not be reversible)
- Slow-down of transfer processes in the brain
- Cancer (caused by high levels of tar and cancer-causing substances, for example, benzopyrene, in marijuana)
- Lack of motivation
- Damage to the offspring

COCAINE

ALL IS NOT GOLD

COCAINE
All Is Not Gold

If a single drug was to be regarded as the 'drug of the eighties,' it would have to be cocaine. Although cocaine has been around for some time, widespread use has only recently become widely publicized. Cocaine initially was the drug of the elite—it was considered a sign of wealth. This is not the case anymore. Many segments of society, including the poor, have succumbed to cocaine. Unfortunately, the dangers of cocaine use have not been adequately portrayed. The movie industry has glamourized the drug and should be held accountable for falsifying the *real* effects. This industry is obviously not telling the true story. The drug does kill. Death can occur suddenly, without warning. Unlike gold, life does not have any glitter if hooked on cocaine.

The following cases depict the dangers associated the cocaine use.

> *Ron, a 25-year-old male, experienced a convulsion after intravenous cocaine use. He had been abusing the drug on an average of three times a day for about eight months. Although the majority of his cocaine abuse involved snorting the drug, he was able to develop an intravenous form of administration which he used during the last month.*
> *At about six o'clock on the morning he was admitted to hospital, he injected two 'dimes' (about 140 mg) of the drug. He instantly felt dizzy and fell to the floor. His mother arrived shortly and noticed Ron was convulsing. Ron appeared confused but alert when seen later at the hospital.*

> *Lisa, a 21-year-old female, went with a group of friends to a party. After drinking several cocktails she snorted a white powder believed to be cocaine. She soon experienced convulsions and*

> *was quickly taken to the hospital. Unfortunately, Lisa failed to respond to treatment and died forty minutes after admission. Several other people at the party admitted using the same substance but denied having any bad experiences.*
>
> *The autopsy revealed that cocaine and lidocaine (a heart medication) had been used.*

> *Jeff, a 28-year-old male, was seen using drugs on the day of his death. He had been drinking early in the evening and smoked two pipes of hashish. Shortly after midnight, Jeff began to snort cocaine and continued to do so periodically for two hours before he collapsed. A friend called the fire department and Jeff was rushed to the nearest hospital but was pronounced dead on arrival. A small vial found near his body contained a white powder . . . cocaine.*

> *Susan, a 19-year-old female, came to the hospital complaining of chest pain. She told the doctor the pain appeared suddenly and that she had no idea what the cause could be. Upon further questioning she admitted to snorting cocaine just prior to getting the chest pain. Fortunately, very little damage was done to the lungs and she did not require hospitalization.*

Until recently, little was heard about the ill effects resulting from cocaine use. The death of the basketball star, Len Bias, in June 1986, brought the issue to the forefront. The first draft pick of the Boston Celtics was dead! His death occurred just twelve hours after signing a ten-year multimillion dollar contract. Traces of cocaine were found in Bias's urine. Other athletes have also been affected and more are now coming forward to tell of their experiences with the drug.

Cocaine is one of the most addicting drugs. Once use is started it is hard to 'kick the habit.' The drug literally takes over your life! Nothing else matters! It has been described as the 'King & Queen' of all drugs.

How Cocaine Is Used

Cocaine is used in a number of ways. The drug is often sniffed or inhaled (snorted) through the mucous membranes of the nose. The cocaine high occurs within one minute when taken in this manner. Nasal problems develop as cocaine is a vasoconstrictor, which means it constricts the blood vessels in the nose. Constriction decreases the blood flow resulting in inadequate nourishment. With continued use, inadequate nourishment could mean ulcer formation in the nasal septum (that portion of the nose which separates the two nostrils) and, if not treated soon enough, ulcers and eventually a hole will develop in the septum. In fact, metal plates for replacement of the septum are available for purchase.

Cocaine may also be injected. The drug, upon entering the vein will travel to the heart, increasing the heart beat and causing chest pain, and heart attacks in some individuals. Disposable syringes are used for injection of the drug along with toilet bowl water. Toilet bowl water is often used for dissolving drugs as abusers have to 'do drugs' privately in order to avoid being caught.

Free-basing cocaine involves the inhalation of cocaine vapours. Commercially, cocaine is available as a salt. The salt portion of the drug is removed by a simple chemical reaction, the 'free base' (that is, cocaine minus the salt) is extracted with an organic solvent, such as ether, and then heated to vaporize the drug. Inhalation of the drug in this manner is like injecting the drug without a needle.

The History of Cocaine

Cocaine is an alkaloid (a common chemical class of compounds) obtained from the leaves of plants such as *Erythroxylum coca.* The leaves contain between 0.5% and 1% cocaine in addition to 18 other different substances. For many years the local inhabitants of countries such as Peru were known to chew the leaves of this plant to obtain great strength and vigor.

Although coca leaves were introduced to Europe by many explorers, coca chewing was regarded as a barbaric Indian practice by the upper-class Europeans. It wasn't until cocaine was isolated from the leaves that interest in the drug became more widespread.

The use of cocaine, for purposes other than medical, began in Europe with the production of a French wine known as 'Vin Mariani' which contained cocaine. The wine was considered to be a sign of social prestige because it was used by the 'upper-class.' In 1886, a second beverage containing cocaine was manufactured. This new mixture was named Coca-Cola. The new drink was popular in North America. In 1906, the Coca-Cola company agreed to stop using cocaine in the drink. Cocaine is now extracted from the leaves, turned over to the government laboratories for medical purposes, and the de-cocainized leaves are used as a flavoring agent.

Recreational Use of Cocaine

Cocaine, as a street drug, is referred to as 'coke,' 'snow,' 'C,' 'lady,' 'she,' 'gold,' 'girl toot,' 'nose candy,' 'white girl,' and 'white lady.' Cocaine users traditionally were affluent people with large amounts of money. To prove their wealth they would often snort (inhale through the nostrils) the drug using a gold-plated straw or a rolled $100 note. The cocaine user today is not just the stereotype movie star but includes blue collar workers, paper boys, students and people from just about every walk of life. Affluence is no longer a criteria.

Street cocaine comes in one of the following forms: coca leaf, coca paste, cocaine hydrochloride powder or free-base cocaine. Coca leaf is considered to be a mild product because the cocaine content is low and it is chewed. This form of cocaine use is not popular in North America because coca plants do not naturally grow in that climate and leaves are hard to smuggle across the border.

Coca paste is one of the first products obtained on extraction of the coca leaves. A high is quickly obtained if the substance is smoked in a tobacco cigarette or marijuana joint. The substance is very addicting and has created nightmares for drug treatment workers. In Third World countries, children have become addicted in a matter of days. Attempts at treatment have not been successful. After release from the treatment facility the person just has to get a whiff of burning coca paste and he's on his abuse pattern again. Because the paste is impure the cost of the substance is minimal when compared to the cocaine hydrochloride.

The hydrochloride salt is the most common form of cocaine sold on the street. This form is also used medicinally for certain types of surgery (eye, nose) as it is an effective local anesthetic (causes a numbness of the area). With street use or illegal cocaine, the powder is most often taken by snorting (inhaling) fine lines of the drug through the nasal passages or by injecting a solution of the salt into a vein. A variety of strengths of the salt are available. These strength differences are accomplished·by 'cutting' the substance with agents such as sugars and starches, which do not have any effect on the body. Sometimes the cutting agents themselves do have an effect on the body, for example caffeine and lidocaine (see story of Lisa at

Crack has its hazards!

the beginning of this chapter) and procaine (another local anesthetic). Final concentrations of cocaine in the samples can vary considerably due to the 'cutting' process. In fact, street samples have been analyzed by laboratories and found to contain anywhere from 0% to 90% cocaine. A lot of street purchasers really get 'ripped off,' paying dearly for something they did not get.

Attemps to remove the cutting agents in order to enhance the effects of the cocaine are accomplished by chemical manipulation and 'free-basing.' Highly inflammable solvents (solvents which explode and burst into flame) are used to extract the free-base (cocaine is a basic substance; the hydrochloride salt portion is thus removed to obtain the free-base). Free-basing is a dangerous practice. Richard Pryor got burned while free-basing. The line sometimes heard, "It's okay to free-base if you don't get burned," is simply not true.

A recent method of free-basing is the instant 'ready-to-use' form known as 'crack' (not to be confused with Crank, an amphetamine derivative). Crack is also obtained by a simple chemical reaction on the salt, cocaine hydrochloride. The substance produced is in the form of 'rocks' which are distributed in small plastic vials. The vials are priced between $10 and $20, a factor which has made them extremely popular. The rocks are put into a pipe, lit, and the resulting smoke is inhaled. The cracking noise produced on heating these rocks is the reason the substance has been termed 'crack.' Crack houses have appeared in many of the major cities of the United States. In Canada, crack has not gained the same popularity possibly due to the advanced warning the country obtained from the United States and the tremendous education provided both in classrooms and by the media. Smoking crack produces an instant exhilarating feeling. The higher the euphoria, the deeper the depression obtained when the effects of the drug wear off. The user knows how to obtain that 'good' feeling again—by using more crack—thus addiction is rapidly produced.

Cocaine Effects on the Body

When cocaine is snorted (sniffed), it is absorbed through the mucous membranes lining the inside of the nose. The membranes try to prevent the drug from entering the body. Blood vessels constrict, thus decreasing blood supply to the nose. This can lead to ulcer formation. Ulcers lead to perforation of the septum (a hole forms in the septum). Some addicts think it is 'cool' to put a handkerchief in one nostril and pull it out of the other. Real magic? The hole in the nasal septum does not heal or fill in because it is composed of cartilage. Surgery is required and a metal plate has to be inserted.

Once absorbed through the membranes cocaine goes to the heart, increasing heart beat, causing chest pain and heart attacks in some instances (see stories at the beginning of the chapter). In fact, the cardiac arrhythmias (variation from normal rhythm of the heart beat) produced by the drug are responsible for most of the deaths—too much stimulation! From the heart, the drug goes to the lungs, back to the heart and then to the brain. The effects on the brain are on a par with human survival factors, namely, food, water, and sex. The drug takes the place of these necessary components in the users' lives. Cocaine effects are the most reinforcing of any drug known to man.

Cocaine interrupts and interferes with the normal functioning of chemicals naturally present in the brain. Normally, these chemicals are uniquely kept in balance. The chemicals are necessary for specific functions. When needed by the body, they are released from storage sites, attach to a receptor, and begin the reaction the brain intended to perform. The process is much like plugging an electrical appliance into a power outlet. The appliance will not function until the plug has been attached to the electrical outlet (receptor). Once the need for the appliance is finished it is simply unplugged or the power is turned off. Similarly, in the brain, once the need for the chemical has been satisfied, the power, so to speak, is turned off and the excess chemical is taken back to the storage site by a 're-uptake' pump. Unfortunately, cocaine interferes with the functioning of this 're-uptake' pump. It fills the cavities in this pump so that the excess brain chemical cannot be returned to the original site—the pump is full and thus cannot retrieve the brain chemical. The chemical is thus left to stimulate the receptor and is not stored for future use. Dopamine is one of the chemicals that is produced by the brain and one that is seriously affected by cocaine use. Supplies in the brain become depleted by cocaine use. Cocaine results in the release of dopamine from its storage sites. As cocaine use is continued dopamine is continually released until the storage sites are empty. It's like squeezing a lemon; eventually it becomes dry. Too little dopamine produces parkinsonism-like effects. The user begins to shake—it's no wonder ball players can't hit a ball and their batting averages bottom-out after using the drug. The brain craves dopamine. Cocaine users take more of the drug in an attempt to squeeze more dopamine out of the storage sites. Eventually there is no more to squeeze. The effects are obviously devastating. Research with scintography has revealed brain damage on continued use. This technique allows the investigator to visualize how blood supplies have been interrupted. If blood is cut off the brain cells will die.

On initial use, cocaine acts quickly on the brain to produce a short euphoric state (feel like you are floating on 'cloud nine') during which the user may experience feelings of great power and overalertness. They do not feel tired, in fact, they feel like they could go on for days. Sometimes the user will turn to other drugs to counteract these symptoms. For example, sedatives (sleeping pills, alcohol, barbiturates, etc.) are used to get some sleep. As the effects of cocaine begin to wear off, depression sets in. The addict may sleep for days or may become anxious and even suicidal if more cocaine cannot be obtained. With frequent use of the drug the addict can become paranoid, oversuspicious and even experience hallucinations. Common hallucinations include sensations of bugs crawling under the skin. Some physicians describe the effect as follows:

"The characteristic of their hallucinations is an arousal of a sensation of foreign bodies under the skin. The first patient scrapes his tongue and imagines seeing small black worms coming out of it. He also looks into the cavities to pull out the cholera microbes. The second patient tears off his skin again, looking in the bottom of the wound to pull out the microbes with his fingernails or with the point of a pin. The third . . . occupies himself looking for crystals of cocaine under his skin."

Although this stage usually develops after months or years of cocaine use, the paranoia and hallucinations can last for days.

Injection or free-basing cocaine produces the same type of effects on the body as described above for the snorting process of administration. Injecting means using disposable syringes (often shared and are a major contributing cause of illnesses, including the dreaded AIDS), and sometimes toilet bowl water to dissolve the drug. A high is obtained within 14 seconds. Intravenous cocaine use may also cause extensive skin damage.

Four days after injection of one-half gram of cocaine into the left arm vein, a 35-year-old man appeared at a physician's office with an infected site on his thighs, an infection that had actually caused cell death. The man had reported that within four minutes after injection of the cocaine he had intense thigh pain and discoloration, followed by bruising and blistering of the area several hours later. He also had a fever and inflammation of the kidney and liver (hepatitis).

51

> *Investigation showed that the intravenous cocaine had pro-*
> *duced clots in the vessels of the skin which restricted blood flow*
> *to that area. This effect was due to the cocaine itself and not any*
> *of the cutting agents. The severe pain following injection could*
> *be attributed to the intense vasoconstrictive properties (causing*
> *constriction of blood vessels) of cocaine and the skin damage*
> *could be due either to prolonged constriction or the direct tox-*
> *ic effects of what was an overdose of cocaine.*

Inhaling the vapors during free-basing or smoking crack gives instant euphoria. Incidentally, there are 'five star free-base chefs' for hire! They reportedly prevent one from getting burned!

Tolerance and Dependence

It is now known that cocaine use does produce tolerance (more drug is required in order to get the original effect) and dependence. In animal experiments, cocaine was injected by having the animal press a lever. In some cases, these animals would self-administer more than 4000 injections of cocaine to a point of severe toxicity and self-mutilation. Monkeys have continued administration until they convulsed and died. A similar psychological dependence develops in humans after continued use. Even a strong-willed character and psychological maturity will not protect an individual from addiction. Soon the large quantities and high-costs of the drug result in financial ruin and possibly turning to crime in order to support the habit.

Reverse tolerance is thought to occur in humans. The process undoubtedly involves a sensitization of the individual to cocaine. This means the body requires less drug, instead of more, to produce the same degree of euphoria. The great danger in reverse tolerance is that the addict has already built up a high degree of dependence to cocaine and is using high doses of the drug. All of a sudden the body recognizes this high dose as too much and the user goes into seizures and may die.

Cocaine and Driving

Cocaine users, after an extended period of use, can become paranoid. In fact, suspiciousness, distrust and frank paranoia are symptoms reported by cocaine smokers and snorters. This paranoia obviously can have a profound effect on driving ability.

The following illustrates how paranoia affects driving.

> *Paranoid to begin with, and constantly suspicious, dealers get erratic if they feel they're being watched. Some will drive ten miles an hour in a fifty-mile zone, then do eighty miles an hour in a ten-mile zone. If this doesn't reveal unwelcome company, the 'coke' dealer still will not relax. Far from it! He might run three or four red lights, hoping this will lure surveillance out of hiding. Some dealers will speed around the block three times, stop the car, get out and wave their arms in the air for what seems to be no particular reason at all. Except that they are paranoid.*

The following true case illustrates the effects of cocaine on driving. It's frightening to think there are people, high on cocaine, who are behind the wheel of a vehicle.

> *A 30-year-old male, with a two-year history of social cocaine use, had been in a treatment program where he abstained from the drug for 90 days. He reported receiving a gift of one gram of cocaine which he used intranasally (snorted) over the weekend. The following day he became overwhelmed by a craving for more cocaine. This was accompanied by depression and suicidal tendencies. Desperate for help, he drove at a high rate of speed to a local treatment center. During the drive he collided head-on with another vehicle, drove from the scene while being pursued, hit a second car which was parked, then exited his own car and ran away.*

In North America it is not uncommon to find cocaine in the blood of some fatal motor vehicle accident drivers. Unfortunately, these individuals are not always just on cocaine. Many have been drinking and because cocaine is a stimulant they do not feel the depressant effects of alcohol and thus drink to excess.

Drug habits are expensive!

Cocaine and Pregnancy

Reports are now appearing in the scientific literature which conclude that cocaine abuse by pregnant women significantly reduces the birth weight, increases the stillbirth rates and increases congenital malformation. The infants also experience considerable stress at birth due to withdrawal from cocaine. The fetus is participating in the drug habit of the mother. Drug intake by the mother results in a portion of the drug passing the placental barrier and reaching the fetus. At birth, the infant is no longer receiving the 'drug' and thus experiences withdrawal symptoms. If the physician or nursing staff are not aware of the drug-taking habits of the mother it may be some time before appropriate measures can be taken to relieve the infant from his/her distress.

As recently as 1980, cocaine was said to be relatively safe, non-addicting and would only cause minor psychological problems. Nothing could be further from the truth! Although the movie industry has, and continues to glamourize cocaine use, we now know there is nothing glamourous about the drug. The happy times depicted are short-lived. This is hard for our youth to believe when they see or hear about their so-called idols using the drug. Cocaine ruins lives, careers, family units, and purpose for living. Death is a possibility either from an overdose (sometimes due to reverse tolerance), a paranoia that leads to suicide or from a traffic fatality. Cocaine is very addicting. **All that glitters is not 'gold.'** The choice is obviously up to the individual. If he could, Len Bias would tell us that cocaine use is taboo.

Health Effects of Cocaine Abuse

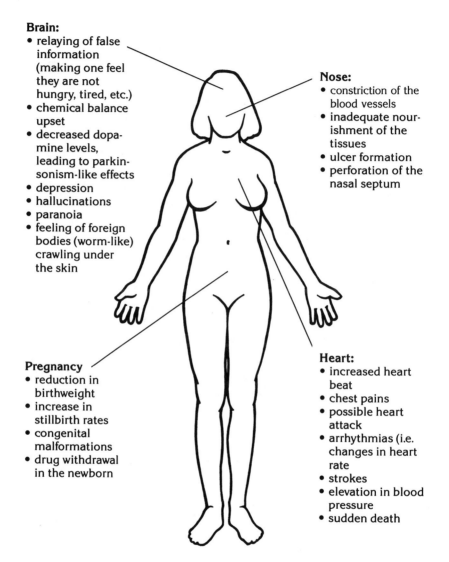

Brain:
- relaying of false information (making one feel they are not hungry, tired, etc.)
- chemical balance upset
- decreased dopamine levels, leading to parkinsonism-like effects
- depression
- hallucinations
- paranoia
- feeling of foreign bodies (worm-like) crawling under the skin

Nose:
- constriction of the blood vessels
- inadequate nourishment of the tissues
- ulcer formation
- perforation of the nasal septum

Pregnancy
- reduction in birthweight
- increase in stillbirth rates
- congenital malformations
- drug withdrawal in the newborn

Heart:
- increased heart beat
- chest pains
- possible heart attack
- arrhythmias (i.e. changes in heart rate)
- strokes
- elevation in blood pressure
- sudden death

Problems Associated with Injections:
- AIDS
- Hepatitis
- Skin infections
- Other infections, e.g. inflammation of the heart
- Damage to blood vessels and organs
- Weight loss (this can occur with any method of chronic use)

PCP
(Phencyclidine)

AN ANGEL IN BLACK WINGS

PCP
(Phencyclidine)
An Angel in Black Wings

PCP or phencyclidine, also referred to as 'Angel Dust,' 'Peace Pill,' 'Hog,' or 'Horse Tranquilizer,' is a dangerous drug; in fact, **one of the most dangerous drugs ever to be sold on the streets**. Although it differs in structure and properties to the other psychedelics in that it causes hallucinations or distortions in perception, it is often taken for the purpose of causing illusionogenic effects (mental impressions derived from misinterpretation of actual experiences) and is thus classified with the psychedelics.

A major difference between phencyclidine and the other members of the psychedelic group is the degree of toxicity produced. Severe adverse reactions and fatalities have been reported. The drug is considered to be extremely dangerous. Only alcoholism, in its final stages, and the continual use of marijuana, because of its fat solubility, have such devastating effects on the brain.

The following factual illustrations demonstrate the dangers associated with PCP use:

> *Mike, an 18-year-old teenage, was brought to the emergency department a few days after having taken what was supposedly LSD. He was brought in because he was extremely agitated. While in the emergency department his agitation increased, he became paranoid and subsequently leaped out of a window. He was retrieved by security guards and sent home with his mother. Twenty-four hours later, he was brought back because his agitation increased, rather than improved. He was then admitted to the psychiatric ward where recovery was realized after twenty-five days of treatment. Only after his recovery was Mike able to recall that the drug he took was not LSD but PCP (phencyclidine).*

Gordon, a 24-year-old man, was observed wandering in the hallway of his apartment building. Dressed in a white sheet, he was knocking on all the doors in the hallway, stating he was Jesus Christ and that he was hungry. His wife gestured to others by pointing to her head, indicating he was confused. Two days later both were found dead lying across one another, on top of the bed. Both Gordon and his wife were known to have experimented with marijuana, however, a subsequent investigation revealed that PCP was the drug responsible for their deaths.

Lynn was a 27-year-old woman who had used phencyclidine regularly over a four-year period. One day while planning to go swimming, she smoked a 'crystal joint' (leaf material, which could be marijuana, to which PCP has been added), prior to entering the pool. While her fiance was changing into his bathing suit, she dove into the pool. Lynn was found, a few minutes later, dead, at the bottom of the pool. Autopsy revealed no head or neck injuries. The only drug present in her body at the time of death was phencyclidine.

Although phencyclidine was first discovered in the late 1920s, it was 1957 before it was realized the chemical had anesthetic properties. As a result, phencyclidine was marketed as a general anesthetic for human use. Unfortunately, physicians soon began to notice that patients, in whom PCP had been used, were experiencing serious adverse effects. The patients, while recovering from surgery, were agitated, disorientated, delirious and experienced visual illusions (a state of being intellectually deceived). Thus, in 1965, medical use of the drug was discontinued. Since then, the drug has been available for veterinary use, functioning as a suitable anesthetic or tranquillizing agent for animals. The serious adverse effects seen in humans are not evident in animals.

It is believed the first illegal use of phencyclidine was confined to North America. San Francisco had the dubious honour of being the city where it all started! The illegal use of phencyclidine was initially short-lived because word spread that PCP caused 'bad trips.' Thus phencyclidine use became virtually absent on the street, at least for a short period of time. Unfortunately, the 'bad trips' were soon forgotten and, in the 1970s, the drug regained its popularity and, once again, was used by many first-time drug abusers for its reported pleasurable effects (a lie used by drug dealers). Despite the undesired effects associated with its use, by the mid-seventies PCP use was considered to have reached epidemic proportions.

For 'street' use, PCP or phencyclidine, was manufactured mainly in illegal laboratories and sold as THC (tetrahydrocannabinol, the psycho-active ingredient in marijuana), cannabinol (another marijuana constituent), mescaline, psilocybin ('magic mushrooms'), LSD, amphetamine, cocaine, or by some other name. This deceitful selling technique was an attempt to camouflage what was really being sold, probably because of the bad publicity PCP had received in the late sixties. It is a bit unsettling that in the mid-seventies one reference reported that *only 3%* of the phencyclidine on the streets was labelled correctly. Many were not getting the drug they assumed they were buying but, instead were purchasing a drug known to totally devastate the brain. These purchases are classified as 'burn transactions'. In other words, it's not uncommon to be sold something other than what you think you are buying—and some of these transactions are **criminal.** On the other hand, others have purchased what was assumed to be a specific drug only to find they had purchased something which had no effect. An example of such a transaction is the individual who bought a capsule sup-posedly filled with mescaline only to discover it was Kool-Aid. A real rip-off! The buyer in the latter incident was fortunate because there would be no brain damage, only the experience of psychological frustration from being ripped off! It deserves mentioning that just because you may trust the indi-vidual from whom you make the purchase, remember that person had to get the drug from someone else, who in turn purchased it from some unknown individual—and so on. Burn transactions are common.

Many drug dealers are trying to make a fast buck. If they can sell you something diluted or 'laced' with such things as PCP to give you a fast trip, they will do it. Millions of dollars are exchanged daily by drug dealers!

In the 1980s, the popularity of PCP grew. As a result phencyclidine is now more often sold as PCP and not camouflaged by some other name.

Phencyclidine Administration

Phencyclidine may be taken by swallowing, smoking, 'snorting' (inhaling it through the nostrils) or by injection. Absorption is rapid and the effects may last for hours or days. The length of effect is determined, to some extent, by the dose. PCP is soluble in fat, thus the drug could be retained by the body for weeks and even months after use.

That inebriated feeling!

Effects of Phencyclidine

As previously stated, phencyclidine effects may last for an extended period of time, depending on the amount of the drug taken. The effects may be conveniently classified under two general categories, i.e. physical and psychological. Physically, dizziness, drowsiness, stupor, variable pupil size, blurred vision, tremors, muscle rigidity, increased heart rate, increased blood pressure and increased respiration may be experienced. Psychological effects include distortion of body image (the person may feel as if he/she has enlarged limbs and a detached head). In addition, an inebriated feeling may exist (like drinking too much). The user could be disorientated and out of touch with reality. Sleeping is not an escape as dreams become very vivid. As the user begins to lose his or her ability to handle and 'compute' the sensory input, messages going to and from the brain do not result in the appropriate response to such things as sensations of touch; heat and cold. The user begins to feel a numbing sensation and eventually no perception of pain. Remember, this drug was used as an anesthetic, and so it's not surprising that you do not feel any pain while under the influence of PCP. At this stage it is very easy for injuries to be ignored.

Agitation and hostility are not uncommon. These effects are believed to be related to individual make-up, rather than to the direct effects of the drug. High dosages of PCP can result in convulsions, respiratory arrest (the person stops breathing) and death. If a coma develops it may last a few hours to as long as days.

PCP, in any dose, but especially at higher doses, may lead to psychotic reactions (like mental disorders) which are hard to distinguish from schizophrenia. Like cocaine, PCP interrupts and interferes with the normal functioning of chemicals naturally present in the brain. Normally these chemicals are uniquely kept in balance. The chemicals are necessary for specific functions. When needed, they are released from storage sites and attach to a receptor, which is the beginning of a reaction the brain intended to perform. Any chemical that is not used by the receptors is taken back to the original storage site by a 're-uptake' pump. PCP interferes with the functioning of the 're-uptake' pump, thus excess chemical is sitting around continually bombarding the receptor sites. This upset in the chemical balance is responsible for abnormal behaviour. Excess dopamine (a brain chemical) has been identified as a contributing factor of schizophrenia.

Speaking of unpredictable, violent behaviour . . .

The psychotic effects produced by PCP have resulted in a number of bizarre-type accidents. The user tends not to fear potentially life-threatening situations. For example, while under the effects of PCP some have been known to try and stop a train, climb into a polar bear's cave to take pictures or jump from windows or cliffs. One abuser even pulled out his front teeth with a pair of pliers (no pain felt), and yet another gouged his eyes while being questioned by the police. Others have committed homicides and suicides (usually of a violent nature). More bizarre stories could be related but would serve no useful purpose.

PCP triggers unpredictable, uncontrollable responses from two parts of the brain—the hypothalamus, which controls rage responses and escape responses, and the cortex, which controls reasoning ability. The result can be an irrational individual who feels cornered and lashes out violently or attempts outrageous acts.

Not all individuals who try PCP will experience all of these reactions but it is important to note—**you never know when a bad trip will occur!**

The pleasant effects described by some users have not been the experience of everyone. A good example of the long-lasting detrimental effects of this drug has been aptly portrayed in the film "Epidemic I." PCP is undoubtedly the most dangerous recreational drug available on the street. The fact that drug dealers are adding PCP to other drugs is the single best reason to stay away from the drug scene altogether. The street terminology for this drug 'angel dust' is quite inappropriate. Angel Dustin, a member of a rock group (sometimes referred to as the PCP Band) is absolutely wrong when he says, "No one would ever commit a violent crime or commit suicide while taking drugs, unless he was going to do it anyway." The alteration in brain chemical balance caused by PCP means abnormal behaviour and abnormal reactions.

PCP cannot be considered an angel, because **angels do not have black wings!**

Health Effects of PCP Abuse

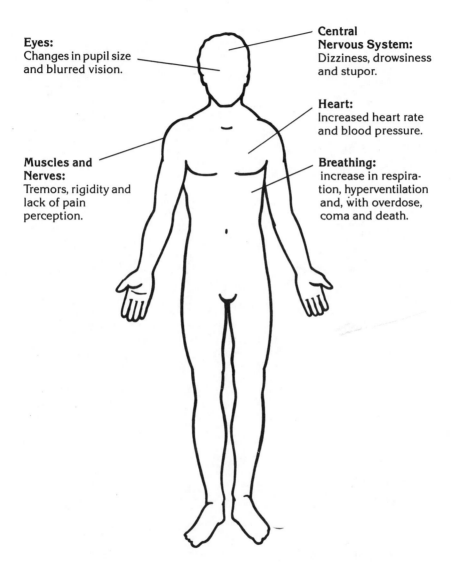

Eyes:
Changes in pupil size and blurred vision.

Central Nervous System:
Dizziness, drowsiness and stupor.

Heart:
Increased heart rate and blood pressure.

Muscles and Nerves:
Tremors, rigidity and lack of pain perception.

Breathing:
increase in respiration, hyperventilation and, with overdose, coma and death.

Psychological Effects:
- Distortion of body image
- Inebriation (drunk-like behaviour)
- Disorientation
- Loss of touch with reality to the point of suicide or homicide
- Vivid dreams ('bad trips')
- Agitation and hostility

LSD (Acid)

YOU'LL GET BURNED

LSD (Acid)
You'll Get Burned!

Lysergic acid diethylamide, or LSD, belongs to a group of drugs classified as the *psychedelics*. Psychedelics are compounds which are known for their mind-altering effects. LSD serves as the prototype (model) drug to which all psychedelics may be compared.

As a 'street drug,' LSD has been referred to as 'Acid,' 'John Lennon,' 'Northern Lights,' 'Blotter,' 'California Sunshine,' 'Windowpane,' 'White Lightning,' 'Wedges,' 'Yellow Dimples,' 'Twenty-Five,' 'LSD-25,' 'Smears,' 'Squirrels,' 'Purple Barrels,' 'Purple Haze,' etc. Probably no other chemical has so many names. Many have suffered severely as a result of using this chemical—**'ACID' does burn!**

The true stories of Murray, Karen and Andrew describe the consequences of LSD use.

Murray, a 10-year-old boy, accidentally ate a sugar cube containing 100 micrograms (a microgram is one-thousandth of a gram) of LSD which his father, a detective, had confiscated from a 'pusher.' Murray had a severe reaction which included coloured visual distortions, illusions and anxiety. These symptoms became less distressing during the following three days, but did not subside. Murray described some of the effects as being similar to having the pain of checkerboards passing through his body.

When Murray returned to school a week later he noticed the pages of books and paper wavered and interfered with his reading. He would become upset while looking at the television because he saw movements without the set being on. A lump would form in his throat and he would cling to his father. Some of his days would be completely uneventful, while others would be filled with visual disturbances. One month after the incident he still saw light halos when his eyes were closed. He was hospitalized and made a slow but complete recovery.

Karen, a 22-year-old woman, was married and had a 2-year-old son. Both she and her husband had used drugs such as LSD on numerous occasions. She also took amphetamines to help deal with her depression. One day she noticed her son was behaving strangely. He appeared unsteady and stumbled. He acted frightened and screamed while looking at the coloured carpet or at the ceiling. He frequently opened his eyes widely and covered his ears with his hands as if to block out unpleasant sounds. Karen suddenly recalled she had two tablets of LSD in her purse and when she went to look for them, she found the purse opened and the tablets missing. The child was taken to a local hospital where the family physician noted symptoms of 'stark terror.' He clung tightly to his mother, screamed at the walls, and would not look at other people or objects. Instead, he appeared to look right through them. He was hyperactive and his heart was racing.

The son was transferred to a children's hospital and given necessary medical treatment. The next morning he appeared alert, responsive to commands and appropriate in behaviour. he was discharged the next day and follow-up examinations confirmed there were no subsequent reactions to the drug.

Andrew, a 20-year-old college student, became involved with a group of drug-using students. They frequently used marijuana, amphetamines, peyote or mescaline and LSD. His involvement with the group was quite regular. Class attendance became sporadic and his academic performance deteriorated but continued to be of passing quality.

One day Andrew took LSD while with some of his friends. He began to pace in and out of the room. Then, without explanation, he disrobed and jumped out a window—to his death!

The above three cases indicate the serious consequences associated with LSD use. Two of these individuals eventually recovered from the

Some experiences can be rather terrifying.

effects of the drug, however, there are others who have not fully recovered and are now institutionalized because the drug actually caused severe brain damage. These individuals appeared to have 'fried their brains.' They are a burden to society because tax dollars are needed to maintain their existence, which in some cases is just a mere existence. If they had not used the drug they would, in all likelihood, be normal, functioning individuals, enjoying life like the rest of society.

LSD was discovered in 1938. In the 1950s, LSD was used experimentally to treat medical conditions such as schizophrenia, alcoholism and homosexuality. Very quickly this method of treatment was noted to be ineffective and thus fell into medical disfavour. In 1965, the illicit use of LSD reached epidemic proportions because of its reputation as a 'mind-expanding' drug. Since then the drug has routinely been available on the streets, although the supply has varied from time to time. For instance, in the early 1970s, an incident in Western Canada substantially decreased the demand. Two teenage boys died from strychnine poisoning. The strychnine was used to 'cut' the LSD. The amount of LSD needed to give a 'hit' is small. In fact, some say, "If you can see the drug it is too much." The drug, therefore, has to be transported in a form that is readily transferable. It is difficult to pass along just a speck of material. A number of the street names suggest ways and means of transportation—for example, blotters or purple barrels. Blotter paper may be impregnated with LSD. Purple barrels are barrel-shaped tablets to which LSD has been added. Unfortunately for the two boys in Western Canada, the method of transportation was to mix the LSD with sufficient strychnine to ease the sale of the drug.

Illicit Use of LSD

LSD is related to a group of compounds known as ergot alkaloids. Alkaloids are basic substances often obtained from plants. The ergot alkaloids are isolated from a fungus growth on the plant *Claviceps purpurea*. LSD is then obtained, quite inexpensively, by chemical reactions on an isolated ergot alkaloid.

The concentration of LSD, purchased on the street, is between 50 and 300 micrograms. Reactions (illusions) will begin with approximately 35 micrograms. Because of the small quantity needed for a 'hit' it is not hard to get a number of doses behind a postage stamp.

After LSD is synthesized (manufactured) it is usually available in the form of a clear, colourless liquid. This liquid is then added to capsules,

An unusual suit-chewing party!

tablets, powder, other solutions such as coffee, paper (blotter acid, stamps), medications such as aspirin (blue dots) or to gelatin squares (windowpanes). In the New England states, LSD has been reported to have been placed on decals designed as temporary tattoos (for example, Mickey Mouse). These methods of transportation are a cause of concern for small children. There was a report of a 'user' bringing LSD home from Europe. He had the clear, colourless liquid camouflaged in a hair tonic bottle. Enroute, the bottle broke, spilling the contents onto the clothes in his suitcase. This did not greatly upset the gentleman. He was still able to hold LSD parties. He simply hung his suit in the living room and had his friends chew on the suit to get their high. A 'suit-chewing party'! LSD is almost always taken orally. Although it can be smoked, the high is undesirable. Other routes of administration, such as intravenous injections, provide equal effectiveness but have no advantage over oral administration. In fact this method of administration adds the complication of dirty needles and the health risks associated with their use.

Effects of LSD on the Body

Some of the changes in normal body functioning are due to LSD stimulating both central and peripheral nervous systems. Noticeable are dilated pupils and an increase in alertness. Some authors have subdivided the effects of LSD into three categories: somatic, perceptual and psychic.

The *somatic effects* (those affecting the body) consist of dizziness, upset stomach (nausea), muscle tremors, muscle twitches and anxiety. These effects usually occur within 30 minutes after ingestion.

The *perceptual effects* (those involving sensory stimulus) consist of visual (altered shapes, more vivid colours and difficulty in focusing or blurred vision) and hearing effects (either a sharpened sense of hearing or haphazard hearing). Unlike a schizophrenic, LSD users usually recognize that these perceptual effects are drug-related. The trip can usually be completely recalled once the effects of the drug have 'worn off.' The perceptual effects usually occur between 30 and 60 minutes after the drug has been taken.

The *psychic effects* (those affecting the mind) include impaired memory, difficulty in thinking and expression of thoughts, mood alterations and feelings of tension or a dream-like state. Perhaps the most dangerous psychic effect results from poor judgement which can lead to fatal accidents. Individuals intoxicated with LSD have received massive burns resulting from long exposure to the sun. Loss of vision has resulted from actually staring at the sun for long periods of time. Others have suffered falls (see story of Andrew at the beginning of this chapter) because they felt they had supernatural powers and would not fall. Some have been killed thinking they could stop a moving vehicle. Homicides have also been reported, but it is questionable whether these were a direct result of LSD use. LSD tends to calm the user and makes them less violent.

After 4 to 12 hours the abuser will usually begin to return to normal, but the effects and the length of time these symptoms are experienced depend, to a great extent, on the dosage of the drug taken.

The usual effects produced by the drug have been described. However, individuals are also influenced by other factors which account for the variability in the 'experiences' described. Mental state and the environment can also influence the drug experience.

Adverse Effects and Toxicity of LSD

LSD is a drug that can continue having effects on the body long after drug use has been discontinued. The reasons and mechanisms involved are unclear. Panic reactions, also known as a 'bummer' or 'bad trip,' are most typical and are probably related to large doses of LSD or to individual vulnerability (variability). Panic reactions, consisting of frightening illusions, feelings of detachment and fear of going insane, are obviously frightening to individuals. In these instances, for some unknown reason, the user does not realize the experience is drug-induced. However, on the positive side, some do realize what is happening and become so afraid that they never touch the drug again. Prolonged psychosis (derangement of personality and loss of contact with reality) may accompany the panic reactions. The outcome of such reactions have been so pronounced that some have committed suicide!

Flashbacks occur less frequently than the panic reactions. They are reactions that occur, perhaps without warning, long after the drug has been used. They can occur from five to 10 times a day and may occur up to 18 months after drug use. An estimated 5% of LSD users will experience flashbacks. These episodes 'replay' all the effects of the drug including visual changes, distortions in the senses, time and reality. Panic attacks, depression and *deja vu* (I've experienced this before!) episodes have also been reported. Although the exact mechanism of flashbacks is unknown, it has been suggested they may be related to abnormalities in brain function, similar to epilepsy. Stress, fatigue and the use of other drugs (for example, marijuana and barbiturates) can precipitate flashback reactions.

Plant Sources of Alkaloids Similar to LSD

Earlier in this chapter it was mentioned that LSD was made by chemical manipulation of an alkaloid found in *Claviceps purpurea*. Morning Glory plants, particularly the seeds, also contain alkaloids related to LSD. It has been known for quite some time that ingestion of Morning Glory seeds can produce effects similar to LSD. The seeds are about one-tenth as potent as LSD. Three hundred 'Heavenly Blue' seeds will produce effects equivalent to 200 or 300 micrograms of LSD. 'Hawaiian Baby Woodrose' seeds are 10 times more potent. These seeds were once available for horticultural purposes, but not for human use. As LSD users became more aware of the 'highs' they could obtain from these seeds, their abuse became prevalent and the seeds had to be removed from the legal market.

The following true cases illustrate the effects of Morning Glory seed ingestion.

Ken, a 24-year-old man, came from a disturbed home environment. He first learned of the effects from Morning Glory seed ingestion in a newspaper article which pointed out the dangers of the seeds. After taking the seeds orally and not finding the 'high' entirely satisfactory, he prepared an intravenous injection and administered it to himself. He described the results as being 'dramatic.' Within seconds he was 'jolted back' in his chair. He experienced a feeling of nothingness and became fascinated with his body movements. His head felt detached from his body and he felt he had to move his body slowly to prevent it from falling onto the floor. He also felt very compassionate, loving everyone and everything.

After 30 minutes after the injection, he developed an upset stomach, vomiting, diarrhea, chills and blurred vision (which lasted for days). He later went into shock and had to be taken to the hospital where he was given supportive medical care.

One month later, Ken reported the perceptual distortions returned when he was tired or distracted. He believed he had permanently damaged his brain. For months later he felt powerfully attracted to the drug. He thought the sensations could be made to return at will, but sometimes recurred against his will. Despite his negative experience, Ken planned to continue using psychedelic drugs.

> *Ron, a 24-year-old university student, chewed 300 Heavenly Blue seeds and experienced an 'illusion type' experience. He became worried when the effect of the drug did not wear off after eight hours. In an effort to alleviate the effect he took a sedative but the experience continued for another 24 hours.*
>
> *For the next three weeks, Ron was somewhat exhilarated with the experience, when without warning, his 'illusion type' symptoms recurred. He denied taking any similar drugs and felt as if he could not control his thoughts. He began to experience ringing in the ears and became fearful of going insane. His symptoms would come and go spontaneously. One morning, a week after the recurrence, Ron awakened feeling very upset. He got dressed, drove his car to a nearby hill, and committed suicide by driving down the hill and into a house at 100 miles per hour.*

LSD (Acid) is a devastating drug, as are the related chemicals found in Morning Glory seeds. It is sad to read about many lives that have been wasted and lost prematurely because of someone selling a 'high.' Because it takes so little of the drug to give a 'hit' one can easily overdose and be 'spaced-out' for a long time. Many LSD users have become so scared or upset with what is going on that they resorted to drastic measures (such as what happened to Ron in the case described above). The number of young people in institutions because of a 'bad trip' is a constant reminder that **'Acid' (LSD)** ingestion is dangerous—**you can get burned!**

Health Effects of LSD Abuse

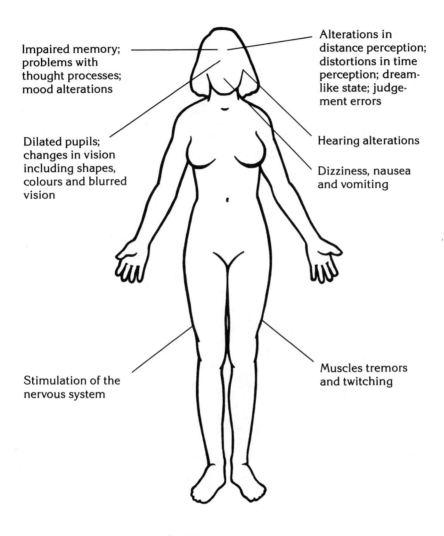

Impaired memory; problems with thought processes; mood alterations

Alterations in distance perception; distortions in time perception; dream-like state; judgement errors

Dilated pupils; changes in vision including shapes, colours and blurred vision

Hearing alterations

Dizziness, nausea and vomiting

Stimulation of the nervous system

Muscles tremors and twitching

- Anxiety
- Tension
- Panic reactions
- Fears of going insane
- Detachment from reality
- Flashback symptoms

* All effects may recur without using the drug!

OTHER PSYCHEDELICS

THERE ARE NO PLEASANT DREAMS

OTHER
PSYCHEDELICS
There Are No Pleasant Dreams

MAGIC MUSHROOMS

In addition to LSD, there are other drugs which may be classified under the heading of psychedelics (compounds which are known for their mind-altering effects.) One of these has been referred to as Hallucinogenic Fungi or, more commonly, Magic Mushrooms. These so-called 'Magic Mushrooms' contain a substance known as psilocybin. Psilocybin and psilocin are the chemical components of the mushroom responsible for the psychedelic effects. Psilocybin is found in about 40 mushroom species which grow in North America, Europe, Australia and Southeast Asia. The mushroom requires warmth and sunshine for growth thus the incidence of mushroom abuse proliferates, at least in North America, during the autumn months, i.e, after a warm summer. In other words, the harvest time for mushrooms is the same as for wheat. One newspaper article titled 'Magic Mushrooms Make Annual Return to City' suggests the mushrooms are a seasonal occurrence. Although mushrooms are considered to be used by the lowest economic strata of illicit drug users, the same article goes on to describe the arrest of a local man who was attempting to traffic 40 kilograms of the drug, with a total street value estimated at $400,000.

Some of the effects of mushroom ingestion are similar to those described for LSD. The following scenario helps to describe the effects of magic mushrooms.

> *Dan, a 25-year-old man, with no previous psychiatric history, was a frequent user of marijuana, LSD and mushrooms. On this particular occasion Dan ingested mushrooms. He had not taken any LSD for several days but gathered huge quantities of mushrooms and began eating handfuls of them throughout the day. He also drank whiskey and smoked marijuana. He began to*

feel 'good.' Colours appeared more vivid and he experienced a
sense of loss of time. Dan estimated he ingested at least 200
mushrooms when he developed a sudden paranoid (suspicious-
ness) reaction and threatened three detectives who arrested him.
When Dan was released the next day, he described having a
disturbed sleep pattern, being irritable, apathetic (could care
less) and experiencing difficulty concentrating. Dan was treated
with tranquilisers and antidepressants for his anxiety and
depression. His condition did not seem to improve. This was
probably because he continued to ingest more mushrooms (50)
on two separate occasions. He declined to be admitted to
hospital and was given an increased dosage of antidepressants.
Dan took an overdose of the antidepressants and had to be
admitted to hospital. Two days later he experienced a 'flashback,'
accompanied by visual distortions. He became panicky, aggres-
sive and smashed several windows before attacking the nurs-
ing staff. He discharged himself but his disturbed behaviour was
noticed by the local police and he was re-admitted. No improve-
ment was seen after two weeks.
Beneficial results were finally obtained by giving Dan four ses-
sions of shock therapy. Dan was discharged after ten weeks in
the hospital.

Psilocybin comes in the form of a small mushroom stock, often pulverized into a flaky powder depending on how dry the mushroom has become. The ingestion of between 20 to 30 mushrooms is the usual quantity required for a 'trip' to last between four to six hours (compare this number of mushrooms with the quantity Dan consumed).

Magic mushrooms may be eaten, either fresh or dried, or they can be taken by sniffing (snorting), smoking or injecting. Injecting plant material is 'loaded with problems'! Much of the material does not dissolve and if injected could cause blood clots.

Health Effects of 'Magic Mushroom' Use

As indicated previously, a number of the health effects seen with magic mushroom or psilocybin use are similar to those of LSD. (The reader may wish to refer to the chapter "LSD (Acid)—You'll Get Burned!" Some of

A Magic Mushroom?

the specific effects of psilocybin reported by physicians are best described by Drs. Peden and Pringle, University of Dundee, Department of Pharmacology and Therapeutics. They describe 44 patients, chiefly school children and unemployed youths, seen at the emergency department of their local hospital after the ingestion of 'liberty caps.' Liberty caps are like magic mushrooms in that they contain psilocybin.

> *Most of the young people came to the emergency department because of restlessness, anxiety and a feeling of an impending serious illness. Four of the patients came because they feared they were about to die.*
>
> *On examination in the hospital, all but four of the above patients had dilated pupils. Some of the patients had heart rates greater than 100 beats per minute (normal rate is between 60 and 80 beats per minute) and diastolic blood pressure of 100 mm of mercury or greater (normal is 80mm of mercury or less). Other symptoms noted in these patients, although not in all of them, included hyperreflexes, flushing of the upper trunk of the body, neck, and face, nausea (vomiting), and abdominal pain. Distortions of perception were very common and these distortions were usually visual (i.e. they were seeing things differently than they actually existed). Some of the patients appeared to be hallucinating. Many experienced numbness, prickly, burning sensations of the limbs and face. Two of the young people suffered from ataxia or lack of muscle coordination. In other words, they gave the impression they were drunk or inebriated. Most of the patients were able to leave the emergency department within one to eight hours, however, they were placed in the care of a responsible adult. Eighteen of the patients actually had to be admitted to the hospital but recovered within 12 hours. The effects of the mushroom ingestion were, in this case, short-lived. They had obviously not ingested an excess number of mushrooms.*

It is apparent that the 'trip' experienced by mushroom ingestion, injection or snorting is not always pleasant. Many of the experiences are upsetting to the individual users. Numerous individuals tell you **there are no pleasant dreams**—a care-free, dream-like state, was *not* experienced.

Beware of the wrong mushroom. It could be poisonous!

A note of caution is necessary in concluding a section on mushroom ingestion. Large numbers of young people have been collecting and ingesting mushrooms from various collection spots throughout North America. These collectors are not trained in the identification of mushrooms or toadstools. Accurate identification can only be made by an expert mycologist (a specialist in the study of fungi) or botanist. The ingestion of a poisonous mushroom or toadstool has to occur only once! The outcome is **death!**

MESCALINE

Mescaline is an alkaloid (an alkaloid is a basic chemical substance of plant origin, although some alkaloids are now synthesized in laboratories) found in a species of the Peyote cactus known as *Lophophora williamsii*. This plant is a small, fleshy, spineless cactus that grows in arid regions of Mexico and the southwestern United States, especially along the Rio Grande Valley. Although mescaline is the major alkaloid found in this cactus there are more than 30 other such compounds. The health effects of these other alkaloids are not clearly defined. We do know, however, that mescaline is the chemical which is responsible for the psychedelic effects.

The mescaline or peyote, available on the street, is available as small button-shaped material known as 'peyote buttons.' These buttons are obtained by slicing small circular portions off the cactus and allowing them to dry to increase their potency. The resulting hard brownish buttons or disks maintain their psychedelic activity even on prolonged storage. The buttons may be softened in the mouth, made into a tea or ground and packaged in a capsule to avoid the very bitter taste. A liquid extract of peyote has also been sold on the street as has a synthetic or chemically prepared product. Unless an intact peyote button is obtained from the distributor of the drug, it is unlikely the drug purchased is mescaline. Analyses of alleged mescaline street purchases have revealed such things as LSD, PCP (phencyclidine), amphetamines, aspirin and even strychnine (rat poison). These examples point out again the uncertainty of purchases made while 'in the drug scene.' Some of them are more potent than anticipated and could be dangerous, while others are simply a 'rip-off'!

Peyote was used in Mexico by the Aztecs in religious ceremonies. In the United States peyote cults began to appear and peyote use in Indian religious ceremonies rapidly became widespread, leading to the formation of the Native American Church in 1918. In this church, peyote-eating is a sacramental rite of communion, and members were exempted from prosecution under the Controlled Substances legislation.

85

Mescaline Health Effects

Approximately 45 milligrams of mescaline is needed to obtain a 'high.' This equates to between four and 12 peyote buttons, although the potency of the buttons is impossible to determine. Mescaline is rapidly absorbed and within one-half to one hour gastrointestinal symptoms such as nausea and vomiting occur.

Other symptoms include diarrhea, excessive perspiration, dilation of the pupils and hyperreflexes along with mild increase in heart rate and blood pressure. After the gastrointestinal symptoms begin to resolve, usually within four to six hours after ingestion, a 'sensor phase' develops similar to that seen with LSD. Sensory phase symptoms include abnormal visual perceptions such as an intensification of colour and geometric imagery, anxiety, emotional upsets leading to paranoia and suicidal tendencies.

Other Psychedelics

There is a group of amphetamines which could be appropriately classified under this heading. The reader is asked to refer to the chapter "Amphetamines—Speed Can Kill."

In summary, the psychedelic drugs are those drugs which have the capability of altering perception by the mind. Some of these effects may appear pleasant at the time, however, the paranoia, suicidal tendencies and the whole problem of the unknown should make one wary of ever trying these drugs. As with any drug, it is extremely hard to stop the abuse once it is started. The whole scene exemplifies the fact there are **no pleasant dreams!**

Health Effects of Magic Mushroom Abuse

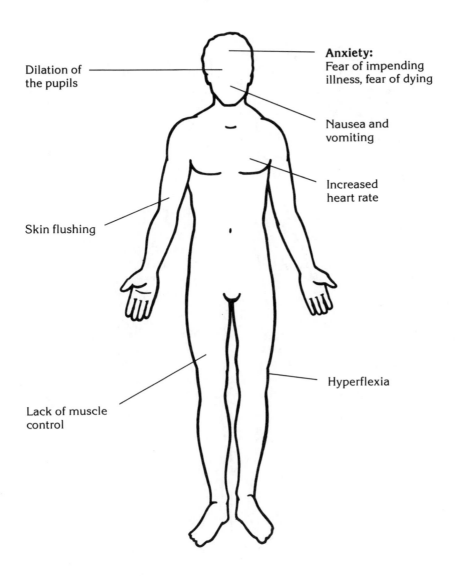

Dilation of the pupils

Anxiety:
Fear of impending illness, fear of dying

Nausea and vomiting

Increased heart rate

Skin flushing

Hyperflexia

Lack of muscle control

- Restlessness
- Increased blood pressure
- Flashbacks

Health Effects of Mescaline Abuse

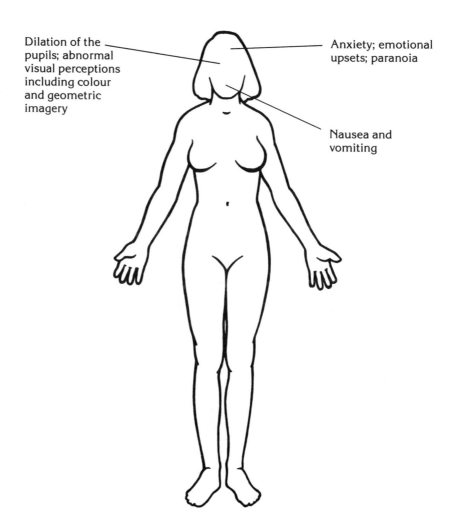

Dilation of the pupils; abnormal visual perceptions including colour and geometric imagery

Anxiety; emotional upsets; paranoia

Nausea and vomiting

- Diarrhea
- Excessive perspiration
- Suicidal tendences

DESIGNER DRUGS

AN ENGINEERING NIGHTMARE

DESIGNER DRUGS

An Engineering Nightmare

A newsletter published by the National Federation of Parents for Drug-Free Youth (NFP), contained an article which opened with the following statement: "Their formulas can be found in almost any university chemistry laboratory. They can be made in any undetectable bathroom-size lab, beyond the reach of customs officers and eradication programs. One lab can produce the world's demand for them without harvesting a single opium-poppy. They are known on the street as China White, Persian White, and Mexican Brown. What are they? **Designer Drugs."**

Designer Drugs became the drug phenomenon of the eighties. They are substances intended for recreational use and are derivatives of approved drugs (i.e. drugs approved for human use). The substances are made in an attempt to circumvent existing legal restrictions. Contrary to popular belief Designer Drugs are not original creations. The majority of these agents are borrowed from legitimate pharmaceutical company research. The drugs represent the most recent developments in the evolution of mind-alterning chemicals. They are marketed under exotic names— EVE, ECSTACY. What kind of impression do these names make?

Chemists, often amateurs, lured by money, manipulate the molecular structure of powerful, controlled drugs to create new drugs not controlled under federal, provincial or state statutes. The proliferation of these substance analogs is phenomenal. These so-called 'new drugs' are quickly made and distributed to couriers, who then sell them to eager, unsuspecting individuals who crave a high. They are told the drug is first-class, potent, synthetic heroin, or some other such name. Unfortunately, these 'new drugs' have *not* been tested for their effects on humans. In fact, they have never been tested in animals. Any new drug prepared by a pharmaceutical company must go through years of testing and millions of dollars in research funds before it is prescribed by a doctor. Drugs take 10 years or more to develop before being approved for human consumption and cost the pharmaceutical company in excess of $100,000,000. It is interesting to note that many potential life-saving drugs developed by the pharmaceutical companies never make it to market. Some unexpected reaction may show up during the preliminary experiments so the drug has to be scrapped. Designer Drug chemists do not have many failures—at least from their perspective.

Designer Drugs have created nightmares for a number of innocent people. Some of these nightmares are depicted below:

> *Todd, a preschool child, walked into his parents' bedroom to wake them. They did not respond to his pleas. They were dead! They had overdosed on a 'new heroin type of drug' (a designer drug).*

> *Carl, a previously healthy 25-year-old man, was admitted to the hospital in an immobile, mute state. His girlfriend stated that over the past eight days he had gradually become withdrawn and had stopped talking and eating. He had a long history of drug abuse. No improvement was observed after an eleven-month treatment period in a psychiatric facility. When referred for neurological assessment, the physician noticed he walked with a stooped, shuffling gait, drooled excessively, spoke in a monosyllabic whisper, and required assistance to feed himself. A diagnosis of severe parkinsonism, of unknown cause, was made. There was no family history of parkinsonism. Carl was treated with anti-parkinsonism drugs and responded dramatically. He was ecstatic! For the first time in a year he was able to speak clearly and to feed himself. He said it was 'like getting out of a cage'. He described 'snorting' a home-made drug, daily, for seven days before his illness. He had made and taken the compound many times previously without mishap, but something went wrong with the experiment in the batch associated with his illness.*
> *Unfortunately, while attending a party on a wharf 20 months after his original illness, Carl fell into the ocean unnoticed and drowned.*

Designer Drugs are not a new phenomenon in North America. In the late sixties laboratories produced LSD and amphetamine derivatives. The late seventies and early eighties brought the potent derivatives of

Death by "design"?

narcotics and other dangerous drugs, causing an alarming situation. One newly synthesized drug just becomes identified and controlled by law then another appears which in turn has to be identified and controlled. A real snowball effect! Government officials have had to deal with federal statutes to close the loopholes. In 1986 the Controlled Substance Analog Enforcement Law was passed in the United States to act as an all encompassing blanket. This outlaws any compound that has a stimulant, depressant or hallucinogenic effect on the central nervous system similar to, or greater than, an already controlled substance or which is claimed to possess these attributes by a seller. Terms of imprisonment of up to 15 years and a fine of up to $250,000 for violations involving controlled substance analogs can be imposed. At the present time (1992), Canada is still dealing with individual drugs as they are confiscated and identified. However, legislation is pending to change the laws to bring them somewhat closer to the United States.

Designer Drugs Related to Amphetamine

The use of chemical analogs for the purpose of avoiding the laws regulating controlled substances was first noticed in the 1960s with the sale of amphetamine analogs. Amphetamine could only be obtained by prescription so it was controlled. However, by altering the structure slightly, 'drug-pushers' assumed they would avoid getting caught. Thus a number of Designer Drugs were manufactured including methylenedioxyamphetamine (MDA), methylenedioxymethamphetamine (MMDA), 2,5-dimethoxy-4-methylamphetamine (STP, DOM), trimethoxyamphetamine (TMA), paramethoxyamphetamine (PMA) and others. These analogs were subsequently controlled by legislation. In the 1970s derivatives of PCP (Phencyclidine, Peace Pill) and methaqualone (the love drug, sometimes referred to as Quaaludes) were discovered, identified and subsequently controlled. In 1982 another derivative of amphetamine, N-ethylamphetamine, became controlled. MDMA (also known as Ecstasy) and MDE (also known as Eve), when analyzed, were shown to be analogs, or derivatives, of MDA (see above) which had been put under the classification of controlled drugs earlier. These two derivatives have similar effects on the body to that of MDA. On July 1, 1985, these derivatives were also placed under the Controlled Substances Act on an emergency basis.

Designer Drugs Related to Fentanyl

The 1980s brought a new group of substances—narcotic analogs. Chemical variation of the parent compounds fentanyl (Sublimaze, Innovar) and meperidine (Demerol) began to appear. Fentanyl is a potent narcotic which, in humans, is about 100 times as strong as morphine. It is used for anesthesia during surgery. Some of the analogs, or chemical alterations to this narcotic have resulted in the production of even more potent substances. So potent in fact that 1.0 gram is sufficient material for 50,000 doses. Other derivatives are believed to be 1000 to 2000 times more potent than even heroin. Fentanyl analogs have been sold on the street as "heroin, synthetic heroin or China White." These analogs have resulted in deaths due to over-dosage. Other unexplained deaths have probably been due to China White but have gone undetected because of the minute quantities of the drug required to affect breathing. For example, one Californian death was obvi-ously due to an overdose of a drug having similar properties to the narcotics. Initial examination of the victim's body fluids revealed nothing. The powder found in possession of the deceased was analyzed and revealed the presence of lactose (a sugar-like substance) and nothing more. Subsequent analysis, using more sophisticated instrumentation, revealed the presence of an unfamiliar product. The substance was not identified until another sudden death case was brought to the laboratory. It took nearly a month to come up with the answer. These types of cases are frustrating to the lay public because things can and have 'gotten out of hand' before the cause has been established. However, when compounds are not available for comparison purposes (standards), many painstaking hours by dedicated scientists are needed before an answer is obtained. Solving the puzzle is particularly chal-lenging when the lives of human beings are at stake. The following true case exemplifies the frustrations experienced by scientists:

Paramedics were alerted to a possible drug overdose by an anonymous telephone call. Upon arriving at the scene, the paramedics found John, a 28-year-old male, with respiratory paralysis (could not breathe). He was taken to a hospital where he was pronounced dead on arrival.

Investigation verified that John had a history of drug and alcohol abuse. External examination of the deceased revealed a well-developed male with a lesion on his left forearm com-posed of yellow tissue and needle punctures. Internal examina-tion showed some irregularities, but subsequent toxicological analyses disputed that the blood contained any alcohol or other volatile components. Nor did the blood analyses show the presence of sedative hypnotics (sleeping pills), barbiturates (e.g. phenobarb), benzodiazepines (e.g. Valium, diazepam), cyanide, nicotine (from smoking), phencyclidine (Angel Dust) or morphine (a narcotic). The urine was tested for morphine, phencyclidine, cocaine, phenothiazines (antipsychotic drugs), methadone (a drug used in the treatment of narcotic withdrawal) and amphetamines, while the liver was tested for benzodiazepines and antidepressants. No positive findings were obtained.

Just consider the time involved trying to determine the cause of John's death. They ruled out all the known possibilities. The list included all the common drugs of abuse usually encountered by their laboratory. Something else obviously caused John's death. Sixteen months later they were able to retrieve the frozen post-mortem samples and determined death was due to a derivative of fentanyl (alpha-methylfentanyl), a derivative so potent that only a minute amount was required for the fatal effect.

Designer Drugs Related to Meperidine (Demerol)

Meperidine or Demerol is another narcotic drug which, when used appropriately, is an effective substance for the relief of pain. Chemists in clandestine or underground laboratories have produced derivatives of this drug which are considerably more potent. In 1982 one analog, known as MPPP (1-methyl-4-phenyl-4-propionoxypiperidine) was identified. MPPP is about five to 10 times more potent as an analgesic (pain reliever) than meperidine. Unfortunately, the process involved in making MPPP must be carefully controlled. This is not the case with samples prepared by the 'underground chemists.' Samples of MPPP, on analysis, have been found to contain MPTP (methylphenyltetrahydropyridine), a neurotoxic substance which damages nerve cells. In fact, this byproduct (neurotoxin) selectively destroys nerve cells in the brain. The brain is not able to effectively handle the chemical dopamine and the individual develops parkinsonism, a chronic nervous disorder marked by muscle rigidity. This disease normally occurs in people over 50 years of age. Therefore, doctors beginning to see young patients with the symptoms of this disease in its advanced stages, were completely puzzled. These young patients appeared in a doctor's office with bent-over posture, slow, almost rigid, movements and had difficulty speaking. It turned out these patients were users of 'Designer Drugs,' or home-made,

Preparation of a Designer Drug.

if you like, narcotics. Some literature suggests the damage produced by MPTP is *irreversible* and appears to worsen with time. Autopsy findings in one death revealed that MPTP had destroyed the nerve cells in the area of the brain that plays a major role in controlling movement.

Other derivatives of meperidine have also produced toxic by-products. Again the synthesis of this drug has the potential of producing toxic byproducts chemically related to the neurotoxin, MPTP. One example is PEPAP.

The problems reported with these derivatives and their byproducts have literally created nightmares for many families and health professionals. On the positive side, if you can call it such, Designer Drugs have resulted in the proliferation of Parkinson's disease. The young patients who have the misfortune of getting the disease will be patients who can be observed clinically for a long period of time. These observations will provide information which will be of value in broadening the understanding of the causes and damage associated with the disease. Understandably, this is a small consolation!

It is disturbing to know there are individuals out there trying to make a 'fast buck' at the expense of innocent individuals. There is no way this kind of practice should be tolerated, that is, developing analogs which have never been tested for activity or side effects before being sold on the street for human use. Young people and adults must be forewarned of the tremendous dangers associated with such practices or there will be many others who will die or become permanently handicapped. Users can never be sure what they are buying from the suppliers. Even marijuana has been known to be laced (or mixed) with potent chemicals so that the user will get more of a 'bang' out of it.

The problems associated with these so-called new chemicals verify that **Designer Drugs are indeed an engineering nightmare!**

Health Effects of Designer Drug Abuse

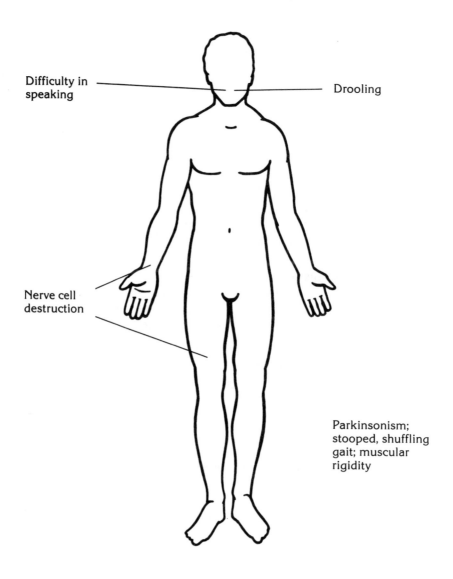

Difficulty in speaking

Drooling

Nerve cell destruction

Parkinsonism; stooped, shuffling gait; muscular rigidity

• Death

*Designer Drugs are chemically related to the narcotic drugs, thus for additional health effects please refer to the chapter **Heroin and Other Narcotics—Beware of Street 'Junk'!**

HEROIN & OTHER NARCOTICS

BEWARE OF STREET "JUNK"

HEROIN AND OTHER NARCOTICS

Beware of Street 'Junk'!

The naturally-occurring opiates, such as morphine, are obtained from the latex-like substance (plant secretion) of the opium poppy, *Papaver somniferum.* Heroin is a derivative of morphine prepared in a laboratory by reacting the plant chemicals with other chemicals. It is thus referred to as being a 'semi-synthetic' compound because part of the structure comes from the plant. It has the greatest addiction potential of the narcotics and is probably the most widely abused of all opiates. A narcotic is defined as a drug that in small doses dulls the senses, relieves pain and induces profound sleep but in excessive doses causes stupor, coma or convulsions. Although heroin abuse was once prevalent only in the adult population, in recent years younger people have become involved. A few case studies will verify that one of the street names for heroin ('junk') is quite appropriate.

Peter had been on the streets since he was 15 years old. Although his arms were like a pin cushion he used to inject heroin under his tongue to avoid the tell-tale sign of the needle marks. He would not admit he had a drug problem.

Charlie, a 20-year-old, started his drug scene when he was just 13 years old, with marijuana, speed (an amphetamine derivative) and acid (LSD). From these drugs he graduated to 'cocktails' of speed and cocaine or a mixture of heroin and methylenedioxyamphetamine (MDA). He then ran away from home and turned to prostitution to support his habit. According to last reports, Charlie was in his second year of rehabilitation.

Ryan was 18 years old when he was admitted to the hospital for treatment of drug addiction. He had a long history of drug abuse beginning when he was just 14 years of age. He started on marijuana but subsequently found amphetamines gave him a lift and would allow him to 'talk for hours.' As the effect of amphetamines began to wear off he felt 'down' and would try to compensate for this feeling by smoking marijuana. At 16 years of age, Ryan started using heroin. Ryan started his heroin habit by injecting a small quantity but soon found he could mix cocaine with the heroin for an even greater effect.

Some time later, Ryan was sent to prison for three months after pleading guilty to marijuana possession. Although he resolved not to take drugs after his release from prison, he resumed drug taking only eight hours after his release. He went back to using cocaine, heroin and speed. Apart from using these drugs himself, he helped and encouraged other boys to inject heroin. Ryan also bought and sold heroin, sometimes 'cutting' it with saccharin to make it go further.

History

China was the first country where the social problems of opium became evident. By 1906, it was estimated that 20% of the adult Chinese population smoked opium and it was further estimated 40 million were addicted.

Opium use spread to the West as a result of two major scientific advances. In 1805 the active components, codeine and morphine, were isolated from the opium poppy. This discovery provided a means for treatment of withdrawal from opium poppy addiction. Little did they realize morphine and codeine were addictive themselves! The introduction of the hypodermic needle in 1843 was another contributing factor to the spread of opium use.

The first of many narcotic addiction periods began in the United States following the Civil War. During the war, morphine was routinely administered to the wounded to relieve pain. When these soldiers returned to civilian life after the war, many found themselves needing the drug to survive and realized they were addicted. This addiction was therefore sometimes referred to as the 'Soldiers' Disease.'

During the nineteenth century, opium derivatives came under strict legal control with the passage of the Harrison Narcotic Act in the United States and the Narcotic Control Act in Canada. Although the number of people using opium-derived narcotics in the United States was quite low in the early 1900s, by 1964 a new epidemic started and has continued.

Narcotic use robs you of good health.

Illegal Use of Heroin

In recent years there has been a sudden increase in heroin use, both in Canada and the United States. In 1983, a study conducted by the Addiction Research Foundation in Toronto found heroin use increased by 1000% from the previous year. During that year Canada spent approximately $2.8 billion on heroin-related problems. Seizures by the federal police force (RCMP) were up by 233%. On the streets of Toronto alone more heroin was sold than the entire country had seen in the six previous years. Heroin was also being used by one in every 70 students from seventh to thirteenth grade. The heaviest use was found in the 14- to 17-year-old age group. Equally distressing was that 12- and 13-year-old students also reported using the drug.

Not only did heroin use increase, but the potency of the product sold on the streets also increased. In the 1970s, heroin was available in concentrations averaging around 3.5%. Products now contain 15%, 20% or higher. China White and Persian Porcelain are two potent substances containing high concentrations of heroin. Sometimes these products are actually some other chemical (for example, Designer Drugs). Late in the 80's more potent products became available which were substituted for heroin by younger people. This results in a faster progression to physical deterioration (remember, growing tissues are more prone to the toxic effects of chemicals than are mature tissues). Heroin abuse is killing more people than ever before!

Heroin usage usually begins after other drugs have been tried. Very rarely does one become a heroin addict as a first addiction. Users generally start by smoking, drinking, using marijuana and psychedlics (such as Acid: LSD). One exception might be persons who have become addicted from related drugs used for medical reasons although physicians and pharmacists try to avoid this from happening.

Three stages of addiction have been identified for narcotic use.

Initial Phase, sometimes referred to as the experimental phase, involves the first use of narcotics. As the individual becomes accustomed to using the drug, they enter the second phase.

Maintenance Phase involves more frequent use of the drug in order to maintain the drug 'high.'

Continuing Phase is the third phase in which the user cannot break the habit because of withdrawal symptoms which are most unpleasant. There is a continual desire, during this phase, to experience the euphoria or orgasm-type feeling the drug provides. In other words, the user is 'hooked.'

Beware of street drug contamination.

Effects of Heroin and Other Narcotics on The Body

Heroin is almost always administered by intravenous injection so that its effects begin, almost immediately, with an orgasmic-like rush, followed by euphoria and a feeling of tranquility. When too much of the drug has been injected a triad of events or three clinical signs occur. These signs are helpful in the diagnosis of narcotic drug use. The triad includes a) central nervous system depression, b) miosis (constriction of the pupils) and, c) respiratory depression. Along with this triad, needle tracks on the arms are also usually evident although Peter tried to avoid this by injecting into the tongue area (see story at the start of this chapter). Often the arms are so badly scarred from injecting, addicts have to use other areas such as the feet, the penis or other parts of the body not already scarred from repeated injection.

Heroin and other narcotics both depress and stimulate the central nervous system, depending on the dose. The individual experiences analgesia or pain relief and/or euphoria effects as well as sedative and hypnotic or sleep-inducing effects. The respiratory centers are depressed. With high dosages, a general excitation of the central nervous system may lead to convulsions. Other effects include: cold and clammy skin, hypothermia (body temperature decreases) and decreased urine output; nausea and vomiting; pupil constriction—usually the tell-tale sign of narcotic use; slowing of the heart which can lead to low blood pressure; and in the severely poisoned individual there is circulatory collapse, heart arrest and death.

Narcotic users are often constipated. This can happen even with the prescribed narcotics received from your physician and pharmacist. The reason for the constipation is a decrease in motility of the gastrointestinal system, caused by the narcotic drugs.

Other serious medical consequences resulting from narcotic abuse include the development of numerous infections including tetanus, inflammation of the area surrounding the heart and inflammation of the liver (hepatitis). Often these complications are a result of using dirty needles to inject or perhaps due to a combination of dirty needles and a contaminated drug. It is very rare that pure drugs are sold on the street. There wouldn't be enough profit for the seller. Pneumonia and tuberculosis have also been reported in narcotic abusers. Combined with all these problems, the overall health of the narcotic abuser is poor. This is due, in part, to inadequate diet and the lack of proper nutrition.

Drug habits are often linked with crime.

Frequently abusers overdose because of the high variability in the heroin concentrations purchased on the street. Many addicts have over-estimated the amount of the drug their body can handle, perhaps because they do not realize the potency of the product they purchased has increased. The user thus quickly passes through respiratory arrest to death. In 1980 there were 850 deaths in the United States directly related to heroin abuse. This figure represented a 20% increase from the previous year.

Tolerance and Withdrawal

The rapid development of tolerance and the severity of the with-drawal effects from heroin and the other narcotics quickly reinforces the con-tinued need for narcotics. Tolerance leads to the never ending need to increase the dose to achieve the euphoric effects and, most importantly, to avoid withdrawal symptoms. Withdrawal symptoms begin within a few hours after taking the last dose. The symptoms include running eyes and nose, uncontrollable yawning, chills, goose bumps and piloerection (the hair on the arms and legs appears to stand up). These symptoms are probably responsible for the term 'cold turkey' which is used to describe someone 'coming off' narotics. Muscle pain and spasms, involuntary leg movements ('kicking the habit') cramps, tremors, inability to sleep, nausea, vomiting, diarrhea, and an increase in pupil size, blood pressure, heart rate, respira-tion rate and body temperature are common withdrawal symptoms. The male addict may experience erections of the penis and premature ejaculation of seminal fluid. The female addict may experience the occasional orgasm. Generally the addict finds many of the withdrawal symptoms unbearable and will do anything to get more drug. In a hospital setting a physician will prescribe medications to decrease the severity of the withdrawal effects.

Heroin addicts rarely attain true abstinence from the drug and will often return to their habit. The relapse rate has been reported to be as high as 80% to 90%. In other words, this type of addiction is very hard to treat and is a real challenge to rehabilitation staff.

Crime Associated With Narcotic Use

The high cost associated with maintaining a heroin habit is often linked with crime. One must realize, however, that crime is not only associated with the abuse of narcotics; the same could apply to marijuana if the user is experiencing a cash flow problem. It has been estimated that 30% to 40% of all heroin is purchased with money obtained as a result of burglaries, robberies, shoplifting and other non-violent crimes.

With respect to violence, heroin is seldom involved. Studies conducted in the 1970s suggest the opiate user is less likely to commit homicide, rape or assault than are the users of alcohol, amphetamines and barbiturates. One study even showed heroin addicts prefer non-violent crimes such as shoplifting over violence. The reason for these tendencies may be related to the tranquilizing or sedating effects of the drug.

Other Narcotics

Most of the discussion thus far has focused on heroin. The opium poppy, *Papaver somniferum,* contains at least 25 different substances known as alkaloids. The main narcotic alkaloids are morphine and codeine. Chemical manipulation of morphine produces heroin, the more potent narcotic. Other chemical manipulations result in the formation of hydromorphone, oxymorphone, hydrocodone and oxycodone. All of these, if taken in sufficient quantity, produce the signs and symptoms described above. Codeine is less addictive and is found in small quantities as one component in a number of prescription and over-the-counter drug preparations. Deaths due to codeine are infrequent.

The above narcotics are referred to as 'natural' or semisynthetic. They are produced by starting with a natural narcotic, i.e. obtained from a plant source, and then altering the structure by chemical manipulation. There are also other narcotics produced entirely by chemical means. The best known example of these is meperidine or Demerol. The addiction potential to this narcotic is relatively high.

Pentazocine

This synthetic narcotic (does not come from a plant source) is less potent than morphine and when first marketed for human use, was considered to possess little or no abuse potential. Unfortunately, this was not the case. Within a short time the abuse potential of pentazocine was realized. The street addicts began to use pentazocine (Talwin) along with the antihistamine, tripelennamine, to obtain a 'high'. The combination is commonly referred to as "T's and Blues." Crushed tablets are mixed with water and injected intravenously.

Pentazocine has created problems for physicians and pharmacists. Drug addicts have tried various means to get this drug. Forged prescriptions are not uncommon. Medical symptoms which would require a prescription for a narcotic have been portrayed by addicts, with surprising accuracy, which has fooled many doctors. Weekends in crowded emergency departments are times commonly used by addicts to try and catch the doctor 'off-guard.' It is often difficult for physicians to keep up with the trends. In some parts of North America, a triplicate prescription plan has been put into effect for prescription narcotics. This has decreased the abuse of these legal drugs. Computer monitoring by the medical profession quickly detects any over-prescribing and abuse.

Unfortunately, the street value for some of the narcotics is high. To support their abuse, addicts will visit physicians for the sole purpose of obtaining a narcotic which they can sell to someone else. Addicts have 'contacts.' In one part of Canada, four individuals were charged after consulting 300 physicians, and obtaining 40,000 narcotic tablets from 1100 pharmacies. The 'street value' of the tablets was estimated to be between $2 and $3 million. Heroin purchased on the street is never pure. It is 'cut' with any number of chemicals. This lack of purity may scare addicts into deciding to turn to prescription narcotics. At least the purity of the product is known.

Narcotic abuse is rampant. When one examines all the serious problems that can develop from the abuse of these drugs, it should make one thankful and proud he/she never started using narcotics or hopefully any other drug of abuse. Remember, drugs purchased on the street are never pure. The price of pure heroin is prohibitive! Not knowing the purity makes over-dosing a real possibility. One overdose is all it takes! If an overdose does not happen, the individual may become ill from the impurities found in the street samples. And what about the needles used to inject the drug? Sharing syringes and needles is know to be the cause of many diseases, including those affecting the liver, blood, heart and brain, as well as being one contributing factor of AIDS.

Beware of the junk! By the way, isn't **'JUNK'** an appropriate street name for heroin?

Health Effects of Narcotic Abuse

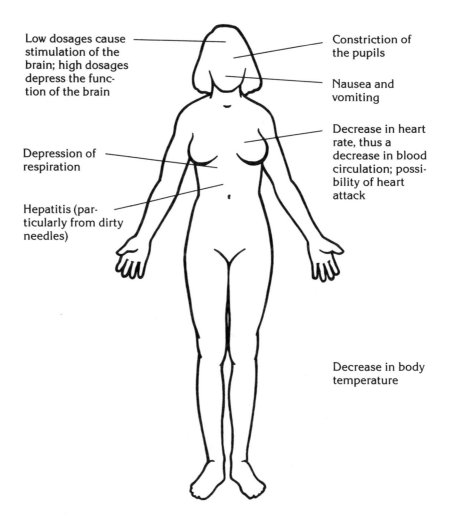

Low dosages cause stimulation of the brain; high dosages depress the function of the brain

Constriction of the pupils

Nausea and vomiting

Depression of respiration

Decrease in heart rate, thus a decrease in blood circulation; possibility of heart attack

Hepatitis (particularly from dirty needles)

Decrease in body temperature

- Convulsions
- Cold, clammy skin
- Decrease in urine output
- Poor health—leading to infections
- Pneumonia
- Tuberculosis
- Constipation

AMPHETAMINES

'SPEED' CAN KILL

AMPHETAMINES
Speed Can Kill

A number of drugs chemically related to amphetamine have appeared 'on the streets.' One of these derivatives, methamphetamine, because of the effects it produces when injected, has been given the designation 'Speed.' Amphetamine itself is a simple chemical compound which was developed in 1887. In 1932, amphetamine was marketed as a nasal decongestant. Soon thereafter, the stimulant properties were recognized and amphetamine was soon used to treat a variety of medical disorders including schizophrenia and morphine addiction. In fact, over the next ten years, up to 39 medical conditions were being treated with amphetamines. In response to the rising trend in amphetamine use, many pharmaceutical manufacturers began developing chemical derivatives of the parent amphetamine molecule.

The initial effects of the amphetamines on the user are to produce wakefulness and alertness, thus making them less tired and bored. Before thinking this is just what you need, please read on! Frequently, users feel they are able to 'take on the world' and are better equipped to perform a number of tasks. One drug user related how he felt his ability at sports was greatly enhanced and that he could not see what harm the occasional use would have. Part of the harm was his conviction and mandatory jail sentence for his drug involvement. This fellow was a young, husky-looking teenager, who had so much potential. Unfortunately, his potential was being robbed by drugs. He would not admit knowing the dangers of his drug habit. What a waste of a good life!

The following scenarios describe effects seen with amphetamine use. One could appropriately report similar symptoms for the other amphetamine derivatives.

> *Rhonda, a 21-year-old female, had been taking amphetamine in large doses over the past six years. The effects of the drug*

gradually caused insomnia (difficulty in sleeping), weight loss and headaches. Before Rhonda was admitted to hospital she was experiencing thoughts of persecution. She became agitated, anxious, disoriented and developed speech problems. Rhonda was treated and released from hospital only to be admitted to another hospital for similar problems a year later. The difference this time was that Rhonda was not using amphetamine prior to this admission.

Even after a whole year her recovery was not complete.

Rick, a 27-year-old pharmacist, was admitted to the hospital two and one-half years after he started taking amphetamine. The drug had been prescribed by his physician for weakness, fatigue and other symptoms. The treatment initially worked in doses of 18 milligrams. Rick developed tolerance to the initial doses of the drug and began taking 10 times the amount (180 milligrams) in order to achieve the effects he felt on that first dose of 18 milligrams. At these doses, side effects developed that included insomnia, weight loss and irregular heart beats. Finally, Rick realised he had a problem with the drug and voluntarily entered the hospital.

After fighting withdrawal symptoms for 12 days, and several weeks of recovery, Rick was discharged from the hospital.

During World War II, amphetamines were frequently used by military personnel. Following the war, use spread to the streets. In the early 1960s, the use of amphetamines, which were prepared by reputable pharmaceutical companies, got 'out of control'. There were too many prescriptions being issued for these drugs. At the same time, there was a significant discrepancy between the number of amphetamine drugs produced by these manufacturers and the number of drugs which were prescribed. It became evident to government departments that these drugs were being distributed by illegal means. In an attempt to partially decrease amphetamine use, strict controls were placed on physicians who wished to prescribe these drugs. There were only two conditions for which amphetamines could be prescribed and these conditions had to be verified by a second physician. Besides this, there was an extensive reporting system put into place which meant a lot of paperwork for the physicians. The

Digging out those non-existent worms!

number of prescriptions for medicinal amphetamines decreased as much as 90% after these strict controls were implemented.

We have not seen the end of the amphetamine abuse on the street scene. New derivatives of amphetamine were, and are, being developed in 'underground laboratories.' These derivatives were probably the first so-called Designer Drugs. These drugs had never been made before and thus were not covered or mentioned in the appropriate Drug Control Acts. Forensic laboratories have identified most of these new designs and, as a result, they are now appropriately covered within the laws of our countries.

Patterns of Addiction

Amphetamine abuse differs from cocaine abuse in that its duration of effect is slower to develop and lasts longer than cocaine. Because cocaine acts so quickly, the effect, or 'high,' is also shorter. An amphetamine 'high' may last for hours. Amphetamine abuse usually begins with the occasional use of small dosages, but as the person becomes more dependent on the drug, it is taken more frequently but still in small dosages. As use continues, the individual may find the need for sedatives, such as alcohol or barbiturates, to relax or sleep. The pattern of stimulant—depressant—stimulant abuse is dangerous. One university student took a stimulant to stay awake in order to study, but needed a depressant to fall asleep. He became sick during the night but did not sufficiently arouse himself to realize what was happening. He choked to death on his own vomit!

Continued use of orally administered amphetamines eventually leads to intravenous use (injection) of the drug. As much as 400 to 4000 milligrams (0.4 to 4.0 grams) have reportedly been injected on a daily basis. Sometimes many repeated injections, called a 'run,' are made to obtain a rush or orgasm-like reaction, followed by a state of mental alertness and euphoria. If this type of abuse continues for several days, the person can become paranoid and may experience delusions of bugs crawling on the skin. This condition is known as formication (not to be confused with fornication). Physicians have treated patients who have tried to dig out these non-existent bugs or worms. Knives or other sharp objects have been used to cut the skin in an attempt to relieve the sensation. The sensation is actually due to stimulation of the nerve endings, rather than bugs. During this paranoid stage, individuals may also behave in a bizarre, violent manner. It is not uncomon for them to commit homicides, smash windows or destroy valuable property. It is, however, impossible for abusers to maintain a continued state of excitation. They eventually collapse from exhaustion and fatigue. The addict then sleeps for days. During this time, depression may become so severe the amphetamine user needs to inject again, as an escape from the depression.

The 'Street' Amphetamines

There are more than 28 different amphetamines which have been identified for potential street abuse. A number of these amphetamines have been labelled by their identifying initials, resulting in what has been described as an 'alphabet soup.' Examples include, MDA (methylenedioxyamphetamine), MMDA (methoxymethylenedioxyamphetamine, also known as Ecstasy) and DOM or STP (dimethoxymethylamphetamine). These amphetamines are synthesized (made) in illegal laboratories known, in drug circles as clandestine laboratories.

The effects of amphetamines are similar to LSD, except that they have an increased incidence of adverse panic reactions.

Methylenedioxyamphetamine (MDA)

Medical reports appearing in the literature emphasize the fact that these drugs are **not** just midly toxic, but **can** cause death!

Tom, a 32-year-old man, was admitted to the hospital in a comatose state. History from his friend was vague, but Tom was a known drug user. He had been at a party where drugs were being used, and was later found in the bedroom totally unresponsive. When Tom was brought to the hospital he had high blood pressure, elevated pulse and respiration rate, and a high body temperature. His body was very rigid and his eyes were abnormal. He had what is referred to as 'doll's eyes.' The physicians responded to Tom's condition with vigorous treatment in an attempt to improve his medical condition. Tom's condition initially stabilised after two seizures, but then he began to suffer from diarrhea and hemorrhaging from the nose. His condition continued to deteriorate. He was taken to the operating room but died shortly after from repeated cardiac arrests. Blood and urine analyses were positive for methylenedioxyamphetamine (MDA).

Tom's case is not an isolated incident. His death closely resembles others reported in the medical literature. Other cases describe how unusual reactions can happen even with the *first* use of the drug.

> *Mark, a 22-year-old Caucasian male, had been using amphetamines, barbiturates and various other psychedlics for one year. One night, he and five other friends each took a single capsule containing approximately 500 milligrams (one-half a gram) of MDA. This was Mark's first experience with the drug. After 15 minutes he had an epileptic-like seizure and lost consciousness. He was rushed to the emergency department by ambulance. Twenty-four hours after the incident, Mark regained normal mental status with no evident psychotic after effects. He was discharged from the hospital three days later having had quite a scare.*

> *Marcus, a 25-year-old male, had a long history of oral and intravenous drug abuse. He had previously taken MDA several times but only in small doses. He accompanied his friend Mark, the 22-year-old described in the above scenario, to the hospital and was not ill at the time. However, shortly after arriving at the emergency department with Mark, Marcus became hyperalert and talkative. He did not appear to develop seizures or breathing problems. He was discharged but returned to the emergency department the next night complaining of 'seeing things' (visual hallucinations) even though he had not taken any drugs after being discharged. The effects lasted over the next 24 hours.*

MDA or methylenedioxyamphetamine has the reputation of providing a 'good trip' or a 'tranquil psychedelic experience,' earning the drug the street name 'love drug.' This type of love one can do without!

Methylenedioxymethamphetamine (MMDA or MDMA)

The effects of MMDA are similar to MDA and so the street name for MMDA, Ecstasy, is quite inappropriate. There is now evidence that this amphetamine derivative causes brain damage, at least in animals. It is true

There are enough amphetamines to make alphabet soup.

that you can not always extrapolate animal data to the human but the fact that MMDA does interfere with brain transmitters (chemicals) should be seriously considered. Obviously humans cannot be used for experimentation to verify the effects seen in the animal. Transmitter depletion in the animal is reversible after one dose of this amphetamine, but long-term use causes permanent breakdown of the nerve terminal.

Dimethoxymethylamphetamine (DOM or STP)

Dimethoxymethylamphetamine was originally given the name DOM to coincide with the major chemical substituents attached to the amphetamine (Dimethoxymethyl). STP, a chemical most familiar as an additive for motor oil, also became a name for this derivative of amphetamine indicating 'serenity, tranquiltiy and peace.' The effects of this amphetamine are similar to mescaline (see chapter on "Other Psychedelics—There are no pleasant dreams"), except that DOM or STP is 40 to 50 times more potent.

DOM usage is associated with a high incidence of panic reactions.

Methamphetamine

Methamphetamine, the methyl derivative of amphetamine, is better known as Speed. This drug is generally taken by injection, producing stimulant effects similar to that seen with amphetamine itself. **'SPEED' CAN KILL** and has! The effects of SPEED are not unlike the amphetamines described above.

Smokable Methamphetamine: "ICE"

In late 1988 and early 1989, Hawaii became known as the trend-setter for **"Crystal Meth Abuse"**. In fact the Star Bulletin and Honolulu Advertiser stated there was concern nationwide that smokable 'Crystal Meth' meant the beginning of a new epidemic. They further reported that "the Crystal Meth was a cunning drug, maneuvering itself from a quick smoke with an energized, long-lasting high to something akin to demonic possession". Crystal Meth ("ICE") also became directly or indirectly linked to one-third of the murders in Oahu alone (Honolulu Advertiser—August 4, 1990). There were concerns that the well publicized dangers of 'CRACK' meant some abusers were switching to crystals of methamphetamine thinking it was a safer drug. But they are wrong! The crystals, also called ("ICE"), are the amphetamine equivalent to 'CRACK' cocaine. "ICE" is heated in the bowl of a pipe and the vapours inhaled. The effects are almost instantaneous—like injecting the drug without a needle! The 'high' lasts much longer than 'CRACK' (some reports suggest it lasts for up to 4 hours; the high from 'CRACK' only lasts 10 to 20 minutes). The higher and longer the 'high' the more severe the depression once the effect of the drug wears off. Some can not cope with the depression and know it can be relieved quickly by smoking more "ICE". This begins a vicious circle leading to addiction.

Toxic effects of "ICE" are similar to those caused by oral or injectable forms of methamphetamine—but may occur earlier. These include paranoia (similar to schizophrenia), hallucinations (that often include the delusion of bugs crawling over the body), and hearing voices that can last for some time after the drug has been discontinued. One abuser describes the voices as if there is no privacy—"it feels like people are reading your mind". No wonder abusers begin to freak out! Patients have also suffered from strokes as a result of over-use of the drug. There have been deaths from simply smoking the drug—one patient developed extensive spasms of the veins which precipitated a heart attack, shock and death. Others have become very obsessive in their behaviour—one young woman became obsessed with keeping her home clean; she even began to scrub the corners of the floor with a toothbrush.

Hawaii was considered to be leading the nation (United States) in the use of Crystal Methamphetamine partially because the drug was coming from the Orient. Although the drug has been detected in Canada, the use is not as extensive as that reported in the United States. This does not mean we should be complacent. The drug is around, available and is probably the most addicting drug ever to reach the streets of our country.

Prescribed Amphetamine Drugs

There are amphetamine derivatives which may be prescribed by physicians. These drugs are perfectly safe to take in their prescribed dosages. Abuse potential is always there, but hopefully being made aware of the potential dangers will prevent the possibility of being caught up in the 'SPEED' trap or with any of the other amphetamines referred to as 'love drug', 'serenity, tranquillity and peace' or 'ectasy'. The truth is—these names are inappropriate, false designations. These names should immediately flag a 'DANGER SIGNAL.'

Health Effects of Amphetamine Abuse

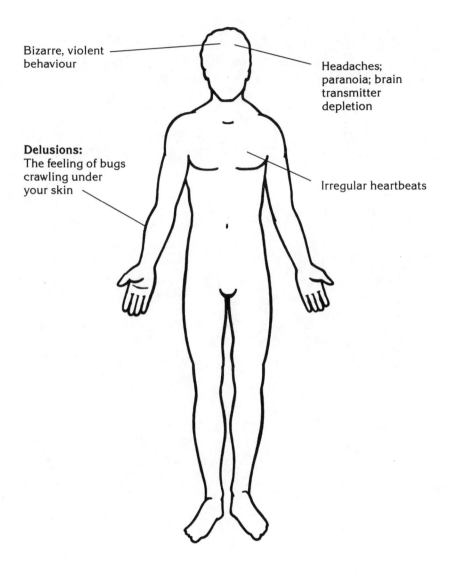

Bizarre, violent behaviour

Headaches; paranoia; brain transmitter depletion

Delusions:
The feeling of bugs crawling under your skin

Irregular heartbeats

- Insomnia
- Weight loss
- Orgasm-like reactions
- Seizures
- Death

QUAALUDE
(Methaqualone)

THE LOVE DRUG?

QUAALUDE
(Methaqualone)
The Love Drug?

Although methaqualone (Quaalude "Ludes") has been described as a "love drug", this term is now more often used for MDA (see chapter on amphetamine.)

Methaqualone abuse has been recognized as a serious problem. This drug, classified as a nonbarbituate hypnotic—an agent that induces sleep—was believed to be the answer to all the problems associated with barbiturates. Deaths caused by persons overdosing with barbiturates and, in particular, barbiturates and alcohol in combination were prevalent. Hollywood abuse of barbiturates was common and led to the expression, 'Valley of the Dolls'—valley referring to the depression which led up to the barbiturate use. It was initially believed that Quaalude or methaqualone would not cause death and better still, the drug did not have the addiction potential of the barbiturates. Medical staff were beginning to breathe a sigh of relief because it appeared that a drug was finally available which would induce sleep and which appeared to be non-addicting. The excitement was short-lived. It was not long before users began to realize methaqualone produced a feeling of euphoria. Methaqualone thus became a popular 'street drug.'

The following case describes the problems associated with this drug.

Charlotte, a 20-year-old woman, was admitted to the emergency department because of seizures. She had taken an average of 300 milligrams of methaqualone daily for several months, but had been unable to obtain the drug for five days. She had used other drugs sporadically, including marijuana and amphetamines, but took nothing except methaqualone on a regular basis. She reportedly only drank beer on Saturdays, consuming two to four cans at a time. Charlotte did not have any personal history of seizures, nor was there any family history of this type of medical problem. For several hours before admission she had muscle twitches in various parts of her body as well as sudden whole body jerks. One hour before admission, Charlotte experienced a generalized seizure with tremendous spasms of the whole body, followed by clonic jerking (a spasm in which rigidity and relaxation alternate in rapid succession) and depression of all central nervous system functions (this would include breathing function). While in the emergency room, a second seizure occurred, with whole body jerks and facial twitches, followed by a sudden loss of consciousness. Charlotte fell backwards, her facial muscles were tight and there was jerking of the arms and legs. She was confused and had recent memory loss. Emergency drug administration by the attending physicians helped Charlotte to become calm, alert and oriented. The emergency drug was continued and gradually tapered off over the next four weeks.

Charlotte did not experience any further seizures during the following year. She did not take any methaqualone during this time.

In Canada a combination product containing methaqualone and diphenhydramine (an antihistamine) was marketed under the trade name Mandrax. This combination resulted in a number of poisoning cases. The combination pharmaceutical product also emerged as a drug of abuse among soldiers stationed in West Germany. There was no clearcut rationale for the combination of diphenhydramine and methaqualone in commercial drug preparations nor was there any known reason why drug addicts would supplement their methaqualone use with excess diphenhydramine. Drug store robbery statistics, where both methaqualone alone and the methaqualone-diphenhydramine product were available, noted increased theft of the combination product over methaqualone alone. Animal studies later revealed diphenhydramine interferes with the breakdown (metabolism) of the methaqualone portion of the medication. This means that higher concentrations of methaqualone are available to reach the brain, producing not only a heightened response but also a greater chance of overdosing.

Abuse of methaqualone has been common since the early 1970s, although the popularity has diminished since the drug is not being prescribed as frequently. Most users now obtain the drug illegally, and so recreational

Seizures of substance.

use continues. Abuse of methaqualone has been worldwide, including the countries of Japan, Germany, Argentina, Australia, Norway, United States and Canada. The drug has been peddled on school campuses and in many urban 'juice bars' where pills are popped with soft drinks.

Fatal vehicle accidents have been reported and often innocent people have been killed. The driver causing the accident appears drunk but no alcohol is detected in the blood. Instead, drivers are 'high on methaqualone.' Court proceedings have shown the drivers get off because they are 'not drunk' in fact, no alcohol was detected. The hands of justice are tied since no laws against driving under the influence of methaqualone are in existence. If a young child, teenager or parent that you know is killed by someone high on methaqualone, how would you feel?

Methaqualone, besides being reported as a drug which causes euphoria, has been flagged as an aphrodisiac—that is, with increasing dosages it increases the desire for sex. This has earned methaqualone the street name, 'love drug' (this name has also been used as a street name for one of the amphetamines) but instead of enhancing, it actually inhibits sexual performance! The drug actually reduces inhibitions and makes one less aware of their thoughts and actions. Other names include 'Heroin for Lovers,' 'the Dr. Jekyll and Mr. Hyde drug,' 'the hottest drug on the street' and so on. The truth is methaqualone is hot—too hot to touch!

Effects of Methaqualone Use

The ingestion of methaqualone will produce toxic symptoms much like those occurring after alcohol or other sedative use. Individuals may appear drunk but the breathalyzer reading will give a zero reading. Individuals under the influence of methaqualone may stagger, slur their words and have a significant slowing of reflexes and judgement. As the user continues to use methaqualone, tolerance will develop. Even though the drug was prescribed as a hypnotic to induce sleep, abusers can become restless and anxious and have difficulty getting to sleep or have a disturbed sleep pattern. Obviously, it is not sleep the abuser is after. Overdose of methaqualone can cause profound depression of the central nervous system and the respiratory system. Death by overdose is not an impossibility, nor are accidents caused by confusion or impaired muscle coordination. Sudden withdrawal from the drug, if it has been used for an extended period of time, can result in withdrawal symptoms which include disorientation, difficulty getting to sleep (insomnia), hallucinations and grand mal convulsions (similar to those described above for Charlotte). Convulsions may occur even in moderate users who abruptly stop using the drug. The body develops a physical dependence to the drug. A report coming out of Florida revealed 246 methaqualone related deaths between 1971–81. The age range of the victims was between 13 and 70 years of age. A number of these were referred to as traumatic deaths, occurring as a result of motor vehicle crashes, although there were a high percentage occurring due to overdose.

The combination product, methaqualone-diphenhydramine, as one would guess, can also produce serious problems. Delirium, hyper-reflexes, convulsions, depression of the heart and the respiratory systems and death have all been reported. Remember, methaqualone is a sedative drug, as is alcohol, so it is not surprising that these symptoms occur with over-use.

If this is what love is all about, who wants it? It is unfortunate that methaqualone and the combination product of methaqualone and diphenhydramine did have potential as effective hypnotics and anticonvulsants, yet the drugs had to be taken off the prescribing lists of physicians because someone began using them to get a high and lied about the pleasures methaqualone is guaranteed to provide. It is true some users have experienced only pleasant effects. Eventually there is a need for more of the drug to continue giving that 'high.' This can lead to overdose problems. Equally serious are the possibilities that the supply will run out, resulting in abrupt withdrawal symptoms. Worse yet, if it could get worse, the wrong drug may be purchased, i.e. a burn transaction. In fact, some sales of supposed Quaaludes were not Quaaludes but PCP (phencyclidine)—one of the most dangerous street drug known to man.

Being aware of the facts will help counteract the false pleasant 'street talk' about methaqualone. **It is simply not true!**

Health Effects of Methaqualone Abuse

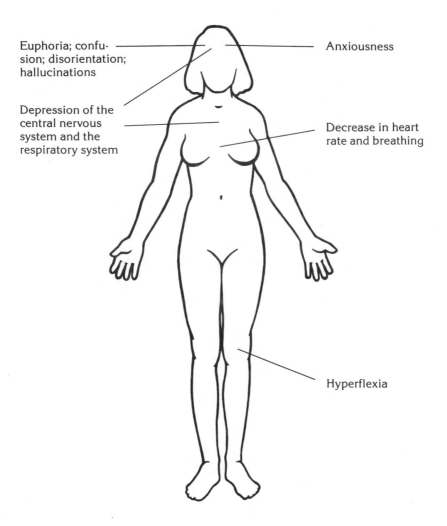

Euphoria; confu-
sion; disorientation;
hallucinations

Anxiousness

Depression of the
central nervous
system and the
respiratory system

Decrease in heart
rate and breathing

Hyperflexia

- Seizures
- Convulsions
- Appearance of being drunk
- Slowing of reflexes and judgement
- Restlessness

STEROIDS

WHY THE RAGE ABOUT 'ROIDS'?

STEROIDS
Why the Rage About "Roids"?

Steroids and sports became big news in 1988 when urine collected from the Olympic sprinter, Ben Johnson, tested positive for an illegal substance. To have his gold medal stripped was devastating not only for him but for Canada, the country he proudly represented. Why did he do it? What are the possible side-effects of such a practice? How do we convince our youth not to take steroids when celebrities have been using them for years? These, as well as other questions, become foremost in many minds. Even though this section will deal with the possible devastating effects of anabolic steroids, it should not be forgotten that these substances are prescribed by physicians, for legitimate medical reasons, with positive results. Medically, steroids are often prescribed for a short period of time with no side-effects. At other times the patient may need the steroid for a longer time. In the latter instance, side-effects do occur which, in some instances, can be disturbing to the patient.

Steroids, if used inappropriately, could produce any one of the following devastating effects:

> *John, a 23-year-old bodybuilder, complained of severe groin pains and was taken to the hospital for treatment. The doctors found that his liver and kidneys had stopped working. He was rushed to the intensive-care unit. Four days later, he died from heart failure. His autopsy revealed he was a steroid abuser.*

> *Bill, a world class power weightlifter with no past history of heart disease was admitted to the hospital with severe chest pain. The pain had awakened him from his sleep. He had been using intramuscular and oral steroids daily during the 6 weeks before developing the chest pain. This athlete had developed*

> *very high cholesterol levels. Steroids, powerlifting and dietary factors may have been contributing factors causing spasms of the artery leading to the heart.*

> *Ken, an amateur bodybuilder was convicted of second-degree murder. Three months before committing the crime he had started taking anabolic steroids on the advice of friends at the gym. He had been assured that there were no adverse effects. Personality changes became evident. Ken became 'hyper' and irritable. He quarrelled noisily and started consuming increasing amounts of alcohol. One night while talking with his girlfriend Ken 'snapped.' His girlfriend was severely beaten and died as the result of a massive blood clot. Testimony at Ken's trial revealed he had become a changed man after he began using steroids.*

> *While Ted was preparing for his high school prom night, he drank a health formula which was promoted as an anabolic steroid alternative which he was using to increase muscle and reduce fat. His evening of romance was not to be. Twenty minutes after drinking the substance he lapsed into a coma. His parents found him on the floor and rushed him to the hospital. The doctors said if he had been found 30 minutes later, he probably would have died.*

The stories of John, Bill, Ken and Ted are disturbing but not unusual. Many athletes will, however, 'push' these drugs because of the increased strength they supposedly provide. This makes them popular to both men and women who want to increase muscle mass and definition. According to the FDA Consumer (September, 1991) abuse is related to the fact that young men feel they need to look 'masculine'—strong and muscular. Young people are not concerned about the long term effects—they just want to make that team and be popular—they'll worry later about the possible damage to the liver, heart and other organs. In fact, most feel they will not be affected because they will certainly stop using steroids before it is too late.

What Are Anabolic Steroids?

Anabolic steroids include the naturally occurring sex hormone, testosterone, and its chemical derivatives. In males, testosterone is responsible for the development and maintenance of secondary sexual characteristics including facial and pubic hair growth and deepening of the voice. In females, where testosterone is present in significantly smaller amounts, it is again responsible for the development of some secondary sexual characteristics such as hair growth in the pubic and armpit regions. These are referred to as the androgenic or 'masculinizing' effects of testosterone.

Testosterone also possesses anabolic or tissue building effects. It promotes tissue growth by stimulating protein production and slowing its breakdown in body tissues.

History and Prevalence of Use

Since the first anabolic steroids were prepared in the laboratory, these drugs have been used to treat a variety of medical conditions. Some of these include the treatment of osteoporosis (a disease characterized by a loss of bone tissue), anemias (conditions in which there is a decrease in red blood cells), hypogonadism (improper functioning of the testes) in young males, and shortness of stature.

Not long after its discovery and isolation in 1936, testosterone was first used for non-medical purposes. During World War II, it was suggested that the Nazis injected their troops with testosterone in order to make them more aggressive during combat.

It has been suggested that as early as 1953 testosterone was administered to Russian athletes in an attempt to enhance their athletic performance. It was not long before athletes started abusing these drugs; some taking 20 times the recommended doses. Abuse led to the development of liver problems in a few of the athletes. At this time, the use of steroids in sports was denounced.

Since the 1950's there has been a phenomenal increase in the use of anabolic steroids by athletes. In 1968, the International Olympic Committee banned steroid use and in 1976, routine urine testing for banned substances was initiated. Prior to 1983, most samples collected underwent what is referred to as 'sink testing'—that is, testing procedures were not very sophisticated and many samples were washed down the drain. Because no one seemed to get caught, testing did not deter athletes from using steroids and use continued to increase.

Because of more sophisticated testing techniques 19 athletes, in the 1983 Venezuela Pan American Games, were disqualified due to detection of steroids in their urine. Testing was now more sophisticated.

The actual number of athletes using anabolic steroids is not known. According to the committee on doping in amateur sport, only 5% of athletes in Canada used steroids in 1980. Other studies suggest that this is an underestimation and have provided the following usage levels—approximately 98% of all male body-builders and powerlifters including Olympic weight lifters are believed to use anabolic steroids. Fifty to 90% of athletes involved in sports such as track and field and football are suspected of using anabolic steroids to improve their performance. These figures are a far cry from the 1980 estimate of 5%.

Over the past few years, illicit use of steroids has become widespread. Elite athletes are no longer exclusive users of these drugs. Users now include both non-competitive athletes and non-athletes, with use beginning as early as Junior High School. A recent study on the prevalence of anabolic steroid use, in American high school students, indicates about 7% of male students are anabolic steroid users.

How are Anabolic Steroids Used?

Anabolic steroids are taken either orally, often in tablet form, or by injection. Approximately 8 milligrams of testosterone are produced by the testes, in the healthy male, each day. Medical doses of anabolic steroids vary depending on the preparation and reason for use. For example, testosterone propionate, when used for replacement therapy, is administered by injection into the muscle in dosages of 10–50 milligrams 3 times a week. Abusers, on the other hand, take megadoses. Some athletes use 10–100 times the recommended therapeutic doses.

> *Paul, a 24 year old non-competitive weightlifter, was admitted into a psychiatric unit after he asked for professional help to quit taking steroids. He complained of being depressed and said that he had considered suicide. Paul felt these feelings were related to his use of steroids.*
> *At the time of his admission, Paul was taking 200 milligrams of testosterone cypionate intramuscularly every 3 days, 100 milligrams of nandrolone decanoate intramuscularly every 3 days, 25 milligrams of oxandrolone orally daily, 40 milligrams of methandrostenolone orally daily, 30 to 45 milligrams of*

> *bolasterone subcutaneously every 2 to 3 days and 1000 to 2000 units of human chorionic gonadotrophin intramuscularly every 2 to 3 days.*

There are three main methods used by athletes and other steroid abusers to administer anabolic steroids: 'stacking,' 'cycling,' and 'pyramiding.' 'Stacking' refers to the simultaneous use of a number of different steroids. Paul (above), was taking 5 different preparations. 'Cycling' involves alternating periods of steroid use with steroid free periods. The anabolic steroid user will take the drugs for a period of 6 to 12 weeks and then take a 'drug holiday' for 1 to 12 months. 'Pyramiding' is when cycles of steroid use are started at low doses and then the doses are gradually increased. These methods are practised in an attempt to minimize side effects and prevent development of tolerance to the effects of steroids on muscle tissue. Tolerance develops for many of the street drugs and users find they need higher doses to get the effects they initially experienced.

Effects of Anabolic Steroids On the Body

ENDOCRINE (HORMONAL)

In females, deepening of the voice, increased growth of body hair, enlargement of the clitoris, decreased breast size, menstrual irregularities and the development of male pattern baldness are all effects associated with anabolic steroid use. Collectively these effects are referred to as 'masculinization.' Some of these effects are believed to be reversible once steroid use has ended. However, clitoral enlargement, body hair growth, and male pattern baldness are considered irreversible.

In men, anabolic steroids may cause testicular atrophy (wasting away of testicle tissue), impotence, infertility and enlargement of the breasts. Testicular atrophy and infertility are probably reversible but breast growth is not readily reversed. In some cases cosmetic surgery may be required to remove the breast tissue.

THE LIVER

Liver damage is probably the most serious consequence of using anabolic steroids. A significant portion of patients taking therapeutic doses

136

of oral anabolic steroids develop liver problems. One can imagine the result of taking megadoses (as the abusers do) of these drugs.

Some specific liver disorders associated with prolonged anabolic steroid use include: cholestatic jaundice (jaundice caused by a blocked bile duct), malignant (cancerous) tumors and peliosis hepatitis (a condition in which blood filled sacs form in the liver).

CARDIOVASCULAR

Due to a negative effect on blood fat, anabolic steroids may increase the risk of developing atherosclerotic coronary artery disease if they are used for extended periods of time. Studies show that the levels of high density lipoproteins (HDL) are lowered and the levels of low density lipoproteins (LDL) are raised in individuals using anabolic steroids. A high LDL/HDL ratio, like that produced by anabolic steroids, is associated with an increased risk of developing heart disease. Remember the story of Bill at the beginning of this chapter!

BEHAVIOURAL

Anabolic steroid use can cause changes in behaviour. These changes are most often seen as increased aggressiveness and irritability. Many steroid users recall at least one episode of unprovoked aggressive behaviour. These episodes are referred to as 'roid rages.'

In extreme cases, symptoms of depression and psychoses (severe mental illness where a person loses contact with reality) may develop. These symptoms tend to increase during periods of steroid use and lessen once steroid use has ended.

Colin, a 23-year-old body builder, purchased a new $17,000 sports car soon after he began a cycle of a steroid use. The payments on the car were steep. When friends who knew that he couldn't afford the payments questioned him about his purchase, Colin told them he had it all figured out and money was no problem. When he stopped the drug, Colin realised that he could not afford the payments and sold the car. About a year later, after starting another cycle of steroids, Colin bought another sports car on impulse. This car cost him $20,000.

> *Darren, 19, was driving home from work one day when he noticed that the driver in the car in front of him had left his left signal light on. Darren found this to be extremely irritating— so much so, that at the next red light he jumped out of his car and smashed the windshield of the car that had the flashing signal.*

MUSCLE/SKELETAL AND OTHER EFFECTS

In children and adolescents, excessive steroid use causes premature fusion of the long bones which means these bones stop growing and full height development is not reached.

Tendon damage is seen in many athletes who use steroids. This may be caused by a large increase in muscle power without a similar increase in tendon strength. The tendon cannot support nearly the weight that the improved muscle can and so it could be prone to snap! Others have suggested steroids inhibit the production of collagen—an important component of tendons and ligaments. Without collagen, the tendon loses its strength and is easily ruptured. A third reason suggested by sports doctors is that the increased aggression, commonly seen in users of anabolic steroids, causes them to attempt to lift too much weight and to be less careful when doing so.

MISCELLANEOUS EFFECTS

Other effects of steroids on the body include 'acne breakouts', water retention, headaches, increased appetite, an increased risk of developing diabetes, and an increased risk of stroke. Steroid users also have an increased risk of getting AIDS and hepatitis B since needles, which are often shared, are used to inject some steroids into muscle tissue. Of real concern is the fact that the body normally produces its own steroids in a balanced fashion. If steroids are taken from an external source, the body recognizes this as being too much and will 'shut-down' it s manufacturing process. If the person requires emergency surgery, becomes ill or suffers any other trauma, the steroids needed by the body are not produced because the mechanism has 'shut-down'. This could result in severe lowering of the blood pressure, shock, collapse, and yes, even death.

Heath Effects Associated with Steroid Abuse

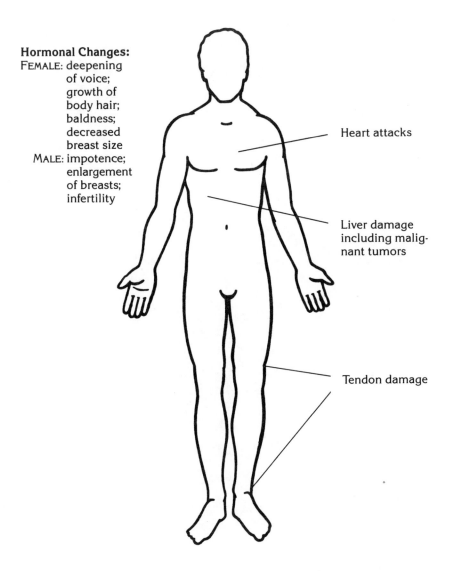

Hormonal Changes:
FEMALE: deepening of voice; growth of body hair; baldness; decreased breast size
MALE: impotence; enlargement of breasts; infertility

Heart attacks

Liver damage including malignant tumors

Tendon damage

- Aggressive behaviour
- Rages
- Depression and psychosis
- Acne
- Strokes
- Diabetes

SIGNS AND SYMPTOMS OF DRUG ABUSE

It is important to note that the following list of SIGNS AND SYMPTOMS are **POSSIBLE SYMPTOMS** because normal adolescent moods often resemble signs of drug use. It is also important that you be aware of any important changes in your child's life so you can help him/her through a crisis. BE AWARE, ALERT AND COMMUNICATE with your children.

PHYSICAL SYMPTOMS

– acting intoxicated
– drooping eyelids; red eyes; dilated or constricted pupils
– abnormally pale complexion
– change in sleep patterns such as insomnia, napping or sleeping at inappropriate times
– frequent illness due to lowered resistance to infection
– runny nose; hacking cough; persistent chest pains
– sudden changes in appetite, especially for sweets (munchies)
– unexplained weight loss or loss of appetite
– neglect of personal appearance, grooming

BEHAVIOURAL AND PERSONALITY CHANGES

– unexplained swings in mood, depression, anxiety and continual resentful behaviour
– inappropriate over-reaction to mild criticism or simple requests
– preoccupation with self, less concern for feelings of others
– secretiveness and withdrawal from family
– loss of interest in previously important things, i.e. hobbies
– lack of motivation, boredom, 'I don't care' attitude
– lethargy, lack of energy, noticeable drop in attention span; short-term memory loss
– change in values, ideals, beliefs
– change in friends, unwillingness to introduce friends
– secretive phone calls, callers refuse to identify themselves or hang up when you answer
– periods of unexplained absence from home
– stealing money or articles which can be readily sold for cash
– wearing sunglasses at inappropriate times

PHYSICAL EVIDENCE

- nickel-sized tin foil packages
- odor of marijuana (like burnt rope) in room or clothing
- incense or room deodorizers
- eyedrops
- rolled or twisted cigarettes (possibly marijuana joints)
- roach clips (devices with a clip similar to a tiny clothes pin on the end)
- powders, seeds, leaves, plant material, mushrooms
- unexplained capsules or tablets
- cigarette rolling papers
- pipes, pipe fittings, screens
- water pipes, bongs (usually glass or plastic and may have brown stains on the smoking end)
- scales, testing kits
- small spoons, straws, razor blades, mirrors
- stash cans (pop cans or other cans that unscrew from the bottom)
- plastic baggies or small glass vials
- drug-related books, magazines, comics (e.g. High Times)
- knives with burnt ends
- propane torch

Many of the above items can be found, usually hidden, in the person's room or car. Some of the more ingenious places of concealment include the underside of dresser drawers, between mattresses, behind light switches, inside stereos, between book pages or in clothing. More obvious locations include car trunks, pocketbooks and closet shelves.

OBSERVED SCHOOL CHANGES

- decline in academic performance, drop in grades
- reduced short-term memory, concentration, attention span
- loss of motivation, participation in school activities
- frequent tardiness and absenteeism
- less interest in participating in class
- sleeping in class
- untidy appearance, dress, personal hygiene
- apathetic
- increased discipline, behavioural problems
- change in peer group

142

WHERE TO OBTAIN FURTHER INFORMATION

Throughout North America there are a number of organizations committed to equipping the parent to counteract the drug culture. To become better informed and to find out where there may be a parent group in your area, call

In Canada: PRIDE CANADA INC. 1-800-667-3747

In the U.S.A. PRIDE (National Parents' Resource Institute for Drug Education, Inc., ATLANTA, GEORGIA) 1-800-241-7946

PRIDE or **P**arent **R**esources **I**nstitute for **D**rug **E**ducation is a resource, information, conference and training institute. Operating on a non-profit basis, PRIDE disseminates accurate, up-to-date drug information to young people, parents and concerned individuals about adolescent drug abuse.

WHAT DOES PRIDE DO?

Trains and motivates parents and community groups for grass-roots action.

Maintains a resource centre of books, publications, films, audio-visuals, and cassettes.

Sponsors annual National Conferences on Youth and Drugs for adults and youth.

Operates toll-free telephone lines. Any person can have immediate access to accurate drug information or referral to professional treatment centres.

Compiles and disseminates accurate, up-to-date drug information in a quarterly newsletter for youth, parents, and community groups.

Provides a speaker's bureau.

Contracts or initiates research on the prevalence and attitudes of drug abuse among youth to provide prevention strategies.

REFERENCES

ALCOHOL:

Depuis, C. et al. Les cardiopathies des enfants nes de mere alcoolique. Arch Mal Coeur 1978; 71:656-72.

Eckhardt, M. J. et al. Health hazards associated with alcohol consumption. JAMA 1981; 246:648-66.

Edmondson, H. A. Pathology of alcoholism. Am. J. Clin. Pathol. 1980; 74:725-42.

Gordon, G. G. et al. Metabolic effects of alcohol on the endocrine system. In: Leiber S., ed. Metabolic Aspects of Alcoholism. Baltimore: University Park Press 1977:249-302.

Jones, K. L. et al. Recognition of the fetal alcohol syndrome in early infancy. Lancet 1973; 2:999-1001.

Lee, N. M. et al. The alcohols. In: Katzung, B. G., ed. Basic and Clinical Pharmacology. California: Lange Medical Publications 1982.

Lemoine, P. et al. Les enfants de parents alcooliques; anomalies observees a propos de 127 cas. Ouest Med 1968; 21:479-82.

Little, R. E. et al. Decreased birthweight in infants of alcoholic women who abstained during pregnancy. J. Pediatr. 1980; 96:974-77.

Loser, H. et al. Type and frequency of cardiac defects in embryo-fetal alcohol syndrome. Report of 16 cases. Br. Heart J. 1977; 39:1374-79.

Lyons, H. A. et al. Diseases of the respiratory tract in alcoholics. In: Kissin, B. and Begleiter, H., eds. The Biology of Alcoholism: Clinical Pathology. New York: Plenum Press Inc. 1974; 3:402-4

Malcolm, J. B. et al. Alcohol intoxication: An underdiagnosed Problem? Arch. of Dis. in Childhood 1985; 60:762-3.

MacDonald, D. I. Drugs, drinking and adolescents: Chicago: Yearbook, Medical Publishers, 1984; 68-72.

McDermott, P. H. et al. Myocardosis and cardiac failure in man. JAMA 1966; 198:253-6.

Morin, Y. et al. Quebec beer-drinker's cardiomyopathy: etiological considerations. Can. Med. Assoc. J. 1967; 97: 926-8.

Morris, A. I. Sexuality, alcohol and liver disease. In: Krasner, N., Madden, J. S. and Walker, R. J., eds. Alcohol-Related Problems. New York: John Wiley Sons Ltd. 1984:251-6.

Russel, M. Intrauterine growth in infants born to women with alcohol-related psychiatric disorders. Alcoholism 1977; I:224-31.

Ryback, R. S. Chronic alcohol consumption and menstruation. JAMA 1977; 238:2143.

Sandyk, R. et al. Transient Gilles de la Tourette Syndrome following alcohol withdrawal. Br. J. Addiction 1985; 80:213-14.

Saskatchewan Alcohol and Drug Abuse Commission. Alcohol, Drugs and Youth - Report of the Minister's Advisory Committee. 1986.

Seixas, F. A. et al. Definition of alcoholism. Ann. Int. Med. 1976; 85:764.

Shanks, J. Alcohol and Youth. World Health Forum 1990;11:235-241.

Shaywitz, S. E. et al. Behavior and learning difficulties in children of normal intelligence born to alcoholic mothers. J. Pediatr. 1980; 96:978-82.

Sokol, R. T. et al. Alcohol abuse during pregnancy: an epidemiologic study. Alcoholism 1980; 4:134-45.

Sulivan, W. C. A note on the influence of maternal inebriety on the offspring. J. Ment. Sci. 1981; 45:489-503.

U. S. Department of Health and Human Services. Sixth Special Report to the U. S. Congress on Alcohol and Health. January 1987: pp. xvii-xviii.

Van Thiel, D. H. et al. Ethanol: a gonadal toxin in the female. Drug Alcohol Depend 1977; 2:373-80.

AMPHETAMINES AND HALLUCINOGENS:

Addiction Research Foundation, Toronto Dial-a-Fact, Transcript 222.

Burns, R. S. et al. Causes of phencyclidine related deaths. Clin. Toxicol. 1978; 12:463-81.

Casey, F. C. Drugs of Abuse—The Facts. PCP—the 'garbage' drug of the streets. Fact Sheet.

Check, F. E. et al. Deceptions in the illicit drug market. Science 1970; 167:1276.

Cohen, S. et al. Prolonged adverse reactions to lysergic acid diethylamide. Archives Gen. Psych. 1963; 8:475-80.

Cohen, S. The hallucinogens and the inhalants. Psychiatr. Clinics N. Am. 1984; 7:681-88.

Dewhurst, K. Psilocybin intoxication. Br. J. Psychiatr. 1980; 137:303-4.

Duquesne University-School of Pharmacy. Pittsburg: The Toxicology Newsletter 1987; 13.

Ellenhorn, M. J. and Barceloux, D. G., eds. Medical Toxicology—Diagnosis and Treatment of Human Poisoning. Part III—Drugs of Abuse. New York: Elsevier, 1988:626-777.

Fauman, B. et al. Psychiatric sequelae of phencyclidine abuse. Clin. Toxicol. 1976; 9:529-38.

Fink, P. J. et al. Morning glory seed. Psychosis Arch. Gen. Psychiat. 1966; 15:209-11

Fuller, D. G. Severe solar maculopathy associated with the use of lysergic acid diethylamide. Am. J. Ophthamol. 1976; 81:413-16.

Herskowitz, J. et al. More about poisoning by phencyclidine ('PCP', 'Angel Dust'). N. Eng. J. Med. 1977; 297:1405.

Hofmann, F. G. Hallucinogens: LSD and agents having similar effects. In: A Handbook on Drug and Alcohol Abuse. New York: Oxford University Press, 1975; 149.

Hollister, L. Drugs of Abuse. In: Katzung, B. G., ed. Basic and Clinical Pharmacology. California: Lange Medical Publications, 1984:353-65.

Hollister, L. E. Effects of hallucinogens in humans. In: Jacobs, B. L., ed. Central Nervous System Pharmacology Series. Hallucinogens: Neurochemical Behavioral and Clinical Perspectives. New York: Raven Press, 1984:19-33.

Hong, R. et al. Cardiomyopathy associated with the smoking of crystal methamphetamine. JAMA 1991; 265(9):1152-54.

Honolulu Advertiser, Feb 5, 1989 and August 4, 1990.

Jackson, J. G. Hazards of Smokable Methamphetamine. N. Eng. J. Med. 1989; 32:907.

Keeler, M. H. et al. Suicide during an LSD reaction. Amer. J. Psychiat. 1967; 123:884-85.

Litovitz, T. Hallucinogens. In: Haddad, L. M., Winchester, J. F., eds. Clinical Management of Poisoning and Drug Overdose. Toronto: W. B. Saunders Co., 1985:455-66.

Mack, R. B. The Iceman Cometh and Killeth: Smokable Methamphetamine. NCMJ 1990; 51(6):276-78.

National Drug Intelligence Estimate 1988-89. Drug Enforcement Directorate, RCMP Headquarters, Ottawa, Canada.

Nesson, D. R. et al. An analysis of psychedelic flashbacks. Am. J. Drug Alcohol Abuse 3:425-35.

Peden, N. R. et al. Hallucinogenic fungi. Lancet 1982; i

Poklis, A. et al. Fatal intoxication from 3,4-methylenedioxyamphetamine. J. Forens. Sci. 1979; 24:70.

Richards, K. C. et al. Near fatal reaction to ingestion of the hallucinogenic drug MDA. JAMA 1971; 218:1826-7.

Shulgin, A. T. et al. Illicit synthesis of phencyclidine (PCP) and several of its analogues. Clin. Toxicol. 1976; 9:553-60.

Simpson, D. I. et al. Methylenedioxyamphetamine: Clinical description of overdose, death, and review of pharmacology. Arch. Int. Med. 1981; 141:1507.

Sioris, L. J. et al. Phencyclidine intoxication: A literature review. Am. J. Hosp. Pharm. 1978; 35:1362-7.

Smith, D. E. et al. The use and abuse of LSD in Haight-Ashbury. Clin. Pediatr. 1968; 7:317.

Solursh, L. P. et al. Hallucinogenic drug abuse: Manifestations and Management. Can. Med. Assoc. J. 1968; 98:407.

Thiessen, P. N. et al. The properties of 3,4-methylenedioxyamphetamine (MDA) I. A review of the literature. Clin. Toxicol. 1973; 6:45-52.

Ungerleider, T. J. et al. The 'bad trip.' The etiology of the adverse LSD reaction. Am. J. Psychiat. 1968; 124:1483-90.

Wessen, D. R. and Washburn, P. Current Patterns of Drug Abuse that Involve Smoking. NIDA Research Monograph 99:5-11.

COCAINE:

Aldrich, M. R. et al. Historical aspects of cocaine use and abuse. In: Mule, A. J., ed. Cocaine: Chemical, Biological, Clinical, Social and Treatment aspects. Ohio: CRC Press, 1976.

Anderson, B. Drug Update: What is 'Crack'? Newsletter of the National Federation of Parents (NFP), Washington, DC.

Ashley, R., ed. Cocaine: Its history, uses and effects. New York: St. Martin's Press, 1975.

Byck, R., ed. Cocaine Papers: Sigmund Freud. New York: Stone Hill Publishing Co., 1983.

Cohen, S. Cocaine. JAMA 1975; 231:74-5.

DeLeon, G. An intervention model. In: deSilva, R., Dupont, R. L., Russel, G. K., eds. Treating the Marihuana Dependent Person. Rockville: American Council for Drug Education, 1981:44-8.

Gold, M. S. 800-Cocaine. New York: Bantam Books Inc., 1985.

Gutierrez, N. et al. Cocainismo Experimental I. Toxicologica general acostumoramieto y sensibilazacion (Experimental Cocainism I. General toxicology, habituation and sensitization.) Rev. de Med. Exp. 1944; 3:279-304.

Haddad, L. M. Cocaine. In: Clinical Management of Poisoning and Drug Overdose. Haddad, L. M., Winchester, J. F., eds. Toronto: W. B. Saunders Co., 1983:443-7.

Hollister, L. Drugs of Abuse. In: Katzung, B. D., ed. Basic and Clinical Pharmacology. California, Lange Medical Publications, 1984.

Kulburg, A. Substance abuse: Clinical identification and management. Pediatr. Toxicol. 1986; 33:325-61.

MacDonald, I. Drugs, drinking and adolescents. Chicago: Yearbook Medical Publishers, 1984.

MacLeans Magazine. The high and crippling cost of cocaine. June 17, 1985.

Maiiani, A., ed. Cola and Its Therapeutic Application. New York: Taros, 1980.

Meyers, J. A. et al. Generalized seizures and cocaine abuse. Neurology 1984; 4:675-76.

Moore, D. C. Complication of regional anesthesia. In: Bonica, J. S., ed. Regional Anesthesia. Philadelphia: W. B. Saunders Co., 1969:217-53.

Newsweek Magazine. June 30, 1986.

Petersen, R. C. et al. Cocaine 1977. NIDA Research Monograph 13. National Institute on Drug Abuse. Washington, DC: US Government Printing Office, 1977.

Shesser, R. et al. Pneumomediastinum and Pneumothorax after inhaling alkaloidal cocaine. Ann. Emerg. Med. 1981; 10:213-15.

Siegel, R. K. Cocaine Use and driving behavior. Alcohol, Drugs and Driving 1985; 3:1-7.

Teri, F. R. et al. The syndrome of coca paste. J. Psychedel. Drugs 1978; 10:361-70.

Thompson, T. et al. Stimulant self-administration by animals: Some comparisons with opiate administration. Federal Proc. 1970; 29:6-12.

VanDyke, C. et al. Cocaine 1884-1974. In: Ellinwood, E. H., Kilbey, M. D., eds. Cocaine and other stimulants. New York: Plenum Press, 1977.

Vilensky, W. D. Q. Illicit and licit drugs causing perforation of the nasal septum. J. Forens. Sci. 1982; 27:956-62.

Weiss, R. D. et al. Pulmonary dysfunction in cocaine smokers. Am. J. Psychiat. 1981; 138:1110-12.

DESIGNER DRUGS:

Buchanan, J. F., Brown, C. R. 'Designer Drugs' A Problem in Clinical Toxicology. Med. Toxicol. 1988; 3:1-17.

Ellenhorn, M. J., Barceloux, D. G., eds. Medical Toxicology- Diagnosis and Treatment of Human Poisoning, New York: Elsevier, 1988:689-762.

National Federation of Parents (NFP), Washington, DC. Newsletters and Bulletins.

HEROIN AND OTHER NARCOTICS:

Alcohol and Drug Use Among Ontario Students (News Release). Toronto: Alcoholism and Drug Addiction Foundation. Jan 5, 1985, in: Alcohol, Drugs and Youth—report of the Minister's Advisory Committee (Government Publication).

Ball, J. C. et al. Absence of major medical complications among chronic opiate addicts. Br. J. Addict. 1970; 65:109-12.

Cohen, S., ed. The Drug Dilemna. New York: McGraw-Hill Book Co., 1969:69-83.

Gossop, M. R. Addiction to narcotics: A brief review of 'Junkie' literature. Br. J. Addict. 1976; 71:192-5.

Heroin Maintenance: The Issues. Washington, DC: The Drug Abuse Council Inc., June 1973. (Second printing; Feb 1975).

Hollister, L. Drugs of abuse. In: Katzung, B. G., ed. Basic and Clinical Pharmacology. California: Lange Medical Publications, 1984:453-64.

Kraft, T. Drug addiction and personality disorder. Br. J. Addiction 1970; 64:403-8.

MacDonald, D. I. Drugs, drinking and adolescents. Chicago: Year Book Medical Publishers, 1984.

Merry, J. A social history of heroin addiction. Br. J. Addiction 70:307-10.

Moore, M., ed. Policy Concerning Drug Abuse in New York State—Vol III: Economics of heroin distribution. New York: Croton-on-Hudson, Hudson Institute, 1970:65.

The Globe and Mail. December 19, 1984.

Toronto Star. January 6, 1984.

Toronto Star. Some kids learn dangers of heroin or cocaine addiction the hard way. November 12, 1984.

MARIJUANA:

Abel, E. L., ed. Marijuana: The first twelve thousand years. New York: Plenum Press, 1980:237-59.

Barry, H. III et al. Delta 1-Tetrahydrocannabinol activation of pituitary-adrenal function. Pharmacologist 1970; 12:327.

Dalterio, S. Marijuana and the unborn. Presentation at the First National Conference on Drugs and Youth, PRIDE Canada Inc.

Klonhoff, H. Acute psychological effects in man, including acute cognitive, psychomotor and perceptual effects on driving. In: Adverse Health and Behavioral Consequences of Cannabis. Working Papers for the ARF/WHO Scientific Meeting. Fehr, K. O., Kala, H., eds. Toronto: Addiction Research Foundation 1983.

Kolansky, H. et al. Effects of marijuana on adolescents and young adults. JAMA 1971; 216:

Kolody, R. C. et al. Depression of plasma testosterone with acute marijuana administration. In: Pharmacology of Marijuana. McBrauded, M. C., Szara, S., eds. New York: Raven Press, 1976:277.

MacDonald, D. I., comp. Drugs, Drinking and Adolescents. Chicago: Year Book Medical Publishers, 1984.

Marijuana—Its Health Hazards and Therapeutic Potentials. Council on Scientific Affairs. JAMA 1981; 246:1823-7.

Maugh, T. H. Marijuana (II): Does it damage the brain? Science 1974; 185:775-6.

Maykut, M. O., ed. Health Consequences of Acute and Chronic Marijuana Use. Oxford: Pergamon Press, 1984: 7-11, 61, 241.

Nahas, G. G., comp. Toxicology and Pharmacology of Cannabis Sativa with reference to delta 9-THC. Bulletin on Narcotics 1972:24.

Ralnick, M. A. et al. Marijuana. In: Clinical Management of Drug Overdose. Haddad, L. M. and Winchester, J. F., eds. Toronto: W. B. Saunders Co.,1983:434-43.

Vincent, B. J. et al. Review of cannabinoids and their antiemetic effectiveness. Drugs 1983; 25:52-62.

METHAQUALONE:

Fraught, E. Methaqualone withdrawal Syndrome. Neurol. 1986; 36:1127-9.

Hindmarsh, K. W., et al. Methaqualone-Diphenydramine Interaction in Rats I: Oral Administration. Can. J. Pharm. Sci. 1979; 14:74-7.

Hindmarsh, K. W., et al. Methaqualone-Diphenhydramine Interaction Study in Humans. J. Pharm. Sci. 1983; 72:176-180.

LeGatt, D. F., et al. Methaqualone-Diphenydramine Interaction in Rats II: Intravenous and Intraperitoneal Administration. Can. J. Pharm. Sci. 1980; 15:64-6.

Pascarelli, E. F. Methaqualone abuse, the quiet epidemic. JAMA 1973; 224:1512

Rosenthal, S. A. et al. Apparent Diazepam Toxicity in a Child due to Accidental Ingestion of misrepresented Quaalude. Vet. Hum. Toxicol. 1984; 26:320-1.

Sangster, G. et al. Medically Serious Self-Poisoning in West Fife, 1970-1979. Clin. Toxicol. 1981; 18:1005-14.

SOLVENTS:

Baerg, R. D. et al. Centrilobular hepatic necrosis and acute renal failure in 'solvent sniffers'. Ann. Intern. Med. 1970; 73:713-20.

Bass, M. Sudden sniffing death. JAMA 1970; 212:2075-79.

Block, S. H. The grocery store high. Am. J. Psychiatry. 1978; 135:126-7.

Brilliant, L. Nitrous oxide as a psychedelic drug. New Eng. J. Med. 1970; 83:1522.

Brozovsky, M. et al. Glue sniffing in children and adolescents. NY State J. Med. 1965; 65:1984-89.

Cohen, S. The hallucinogens and the inhalants. Psychiatr. Clinics of N. Am. 1984; 7:681-8.

Comstock, E. F. et al. Medical evaluation of inhalant abusers. In: Sharp, C. W., Drehm, M. L., eds. Review of inhalants: euphoria to dysfunction. Rockville: NIDA Research Monograph 15, 1977; 54.

Cox, T. C. et al. Drugs and drug abuse: a reference text. Toronto: Alcoholism and Drug Addiction Research Foundation, 1983;74, 295.

Danto, B. L. A bag full of laughs. Am. J. Psychiatry. 1978; 121:612-13.

Di Maio et al. Four deaths resulting from abuse of nitrous oxide. J. Forensic Sci. 1978; 23:169-72.

Fejer, D. et al. Changes in the patterns of drug use in two Canadian cities: Toronto and Halifax. Int. J. Addict. 1972; 7:467-79.

Gruener, N. et al. Methemoglobinemia induced by transplacental passage of nitrites in rats. Bull. Environ. Contam. Toxicol. 1973; 9:44-8.

Haley, T. J. Review of the physiological effects of amyl, butyl and isobutyl nitrites. Clin. Toxicol. 1980; 16:317-29.

Henry, S. The lunch-hour drug and other legal highs. McLeans 1979, July 2:10-12.

Hindmarsh, K. W. et al. Solvent and aerosol abuse. Can. Pharm. J. 1980; 113:99-102.

Hindmarsh, K. W. et al. Solvent abuse-attitudes and knowledge among Saskatchewan retailers. Int. J. Addict. 1983; 18:139-42.

Jager, M. Native gas-sniffing habit brings Ottawa onto scene. Toronto: Addiction Research Foundation. The Journal 1976; August 1:1.

Kamm, R. C. Fatal arrhythmia following deodorant inhalant. Forensic Sci. 1975; 5:91-3.

Law, N. R. et al. Gasoline—sniffing by an adult. JAMA 1968; 204:144-6.

Linder, R. L. et al. Solvent sniffing: a continuing problem among youth. J. Drug Educ. 1974; 4:469-73.

Litt, I. F. et al. Danger . . . vaor harmful: Spot-remover sniffing. New Engl. J. Med. 1969; 218:543-4.

Maickel, R. P. et al. Acute toxicity of butyl nitrites and butyl alcohols. Res. Commun. Chem. Pathol. Pharmacol. 1979; 26:75-83.

McFadden, D. P. et al. Butyl nitrites—an example of hazardous noncontrolled recreational drugs. Res. Commun. Subst. Abuse. 1982; 3:233-36.

Oh, S. J. et al. Giant axonal swelling in 'huffer's' neuropathy. Arch. Neurol. 1976; 33:583-6.

Porter, M. R. et al. Drug use in Anchorage, Alaska. JAMA 1973; 223:657-64.

Powars, D. Aplastic anemia secondary to glue sniffing. New Eng. J. Med. 1965; 273:700-2.

Reinhardt, C. F. et al. Epinephrine-induced cardiac arrhythmia potential of some common industrial solvents. J. Occup. Med. 1973; 15:953-55.

Schmitt, R. C. et al. Gasoline sniffing in children leading to severe burn injury. J. Pediatr. 1972; 80:1021-22.

Sigell, L. T. et al. Popping and snorting of volatile nitrites: a current fad for getting high. Am. J. Psychiatry. 1978; 135:1216-18.

Simmons, R. C. Accentuate the positive in drug education. Health Education. October 1980; 4-6.

Smart, R. G. et al. Six years of cross-sectional surveys of student drug use in Toronto. Bull. Narcotics. 1975; 27:11-22.

Walter, P. V. et al. Glue sniffing: the continuing menace. Drug Forum. 1977. 5:193-97.

Wason, S. et al. Isobutyl nitrite toxicity by ingestion. Ann. Intern. Med. 1980; 92:637-8.

Watson, J. M. Solvent abuse by children and young adults: a review. Br. J. Addition. 1980; 75:27-36.

Weston, M. et al. Youth health and lifestyles, a report of work in progress: Regina, Saskatchewan. Saskatchewan Health and University of Regina, 1980, p.43.

Wyse, D. G. Deliberate inhalation of volatile hydrocarbons: a review. Can. Med. Assoc. J. 1973; 108:71-4.

STEROIDS

Bahrke, M. S. et al. Psychological and behavioral effects of endogenous testosterone levels and anabolic-androgenic steroids among males. Sports Medicine 1990; 10 (5):303-337.

Brower, K. J. et al. Evidence for physical and psychological dependence on anabolic-androgenic steroids in eight weight lifters. Am. J. Psychiatry 1990; 147(4):510-512.

Brower, K. J. et al. Anabolic-androgenic steroid dependence. J. Clin. Psychiatry 1989; 50(1):31-33.

Conacher, G. N. et al. Violent crime possibly associated with anabolic steroid use. Am. J. Psychiatry 1989; 146(5):679.

Derken, G. Bureau of Voluntary Compliance Seminar. NABP 84th Annual Meeting, San Antonio, Texas. May 7, 1988.

Desgagne, M. Anabolic steroids: Use and Abuse Profile in Canada. CPJ 1989; 122(8):402-408.

Goldman, B. Death in the locker room: steroids and sports. Iscarus Press, South Bend, Indiana. 1984.

Goldfien, A. The gonadal hormones and inhibitors. In: Katzung, B. G., ed. Basic and Clinical Pharmacology, 4th ed. Appelton and Lange, Connecticut. 1989; 493-516.

Hickson, R. C. et al. Adverse effects of anabolic steroids. Med. Toxicol.: Adverse Drug Exp. 1989; 4(4):254-271.

Hough, D. O. Anabolic steroids and ergogenic aids. AFP 1990; 41(4):1157-1164.

Johnson, M. D. et al. Anabolic steroid use by male adolescents. Pediatrics 1989; 83(6):921-924.

Kashkin, K. B. et al. Hooked on hormones? An anabolic steroid addiction hypothesis. JAMA 1989; 262(22):3166-3170.

Lorimer, D. A. et al. Cardiac dysfunction in athletes receiving anabolic steroids. DICP, The Annals of Pharmacotherapy 1990; 24:1060-1061.

McNutt, R. A. et al. Acute myocardial infarct in a 22 year old world class weight lifter using anabolic steroids. American Journal of Cardiology 1988; 62:614.

Mottram, D. R. Anabolic steroids. In: Drugs in Sport. Human Kinetic Books. Campaign, Illinois. 1988;59-78.

Nuwer, H. Steroids (a pamphlet). Franklin Watts, New York. 1990.

Pope, H. G. Jr. et al. Affective and psychotic symptoms associated with anabolic steroid use. Am. J. Psychiatry 1988; 145(4):487-490.

Schoepp, G. The storm over anabolic steroids. Drug Merchandising May 1989: 28-32.

Science 1972; 176: 1399-1403.

Streator, S. et al. Anabolic steroid abuse and dependence. PharmAlert 1990; 19(2).

Terney, R. et al. The use of anabolic steroids in high school students. AJDC 1990; 144:99-103.

Voy, R. Illicit drugs and the athlete. American Pharmacy 1986; NS26(11):39-45.